HEAL YESTERDAY'S TRAUMA

FIND YOUR INNER HAPPINESS

HEAL YESTERDAY'S TRAUMA

*Let go of lingering hurt from
betrayal, abuse, harm or grief*

Jennie Bayliss

Troubador Publishing Ltd
Unit E2 Airfield Business Park
Harrison Road, Market Harborough
Leicestershire LE16 7UL
Tel: 0116 279 2299
Email: books@troubador.co.uk
Web: www.troubador.co.uk/matador

ISBN 978 1 80514 113 6

British Library Cataloguing in Publication Data.
A catalogue record for this book is available from the British Library.

Printed and bound by CPI Group (UK) Ltd, Croydon, CR0 4YY
Typeset in 10pt Georgia by Troubador Publishing Ltd, Leicester, UK
Cover and page design by Jennie Bayliss

♥

For my sweethearts.

Thank you for the happiness you bring into my life.

Author's Note

None of the ideas, recommendations and exercises in this book are a replacement for therapy. Before embarking on any of my suggestions, please consider your circumstances. Always take the greatest care to look after your precious body, heart, mind and soul.

While researching client stories, I reviewed my notes from that time. Conversations in the stories that follow are not a verbatim transcript. Rather, they capture the essence of what my clients said and how they shared their story with me. Clients' names, physical attributes, and geographical locations have been changed to protect their identities.

I have made similar identity changes to those mentioned in my stories, except for Joel Young. After reading the chapter, *My story: Forgiving Granddad*, Joel kindly gave me his permission to be included in this book.

Contents

Preface

When one door of happiness closes, another opens;
but often we look so long at the closed door
that we do not see the one which has opened for us.
♥ Helen Keller

'Hi—just wanted to say I enjoyed your talk. You are so lucky to have been blessed in life. I wish I had been as lucky as you.'

Lucky?

The woman speaking to me was dressed in a pale blue shift dress and matching jacket. Her grey hair, loosely pulled back and twisted into a bun, was at odds with her unlined face. My guess was she was in her forties.

For a moment, I was baffled—*what a strange thing to say*—but recovered quickly with a smile. I thanked the lady and replied, although precisely what I said, I no longer remember. Then I turned, walked through the door, down the stairs, out of the venue and into the fresh air. I was in Poundbury, the newly built village on the edge of Dorchester, which, in part, was designed by Prince—now King—Charles. I walked over to my car. On the 30-minute drive home, I mulled over why her words had rattled me.

I had arrived at the venue at eleven and Amy, the workshop leader, came over to welcome me. Around two dozen women milled around the tea and coffee table. Amy soon ushered them back to the comfy sofas, tub seating and padded conference chairs.

Amy is a wonderfully empowering woman. A few weeks earlier, she had called me to ask if I would be a guest speaker at her workshop. Amy told me it was to inspire women to start a business. She asked if my talk could be about how I became a Life Coach, rather than give a personal development presentation. And I had readily agreed.

The women sat balancing white china tea cups and saucers on their laps, chatting to one another, but as I stood up, they quietened and gazed at me expectantly. Over the years, I have given many talks, but speaking about my life felt slightly odd. Amy knew much of my story. I suspected her invitation was to show how some career paths to business are not conventional. Mine certainly wasn't.

I took a breath, smiled and began.

'I have been blessed with an unusual life, including living and working in four different countries.'

Then, for the next fifteen minutes, I shared a whistle-stop tour of my work life. I briefly touched on the early years of studying hotel and catering management in Leicester, then, much to my parents' dismay, I became a nanny in Paris. I zipped quickly through the next few years—my return to the UK and joining the London Hilton where I had met my Japanese husband. I told the women how his promotions with Hilton International had taken us to the Far East—to Jakarta in Indonesia, then to Singapore and finally to Kobe in Japan.

The next few years were more relevant to business, so I spoke about learning basic marketing and sales skills through voluntary work I did for WWF Indonesia. While we were in Singapore, I discovered how to promote my classes to teach kiddies how to swim. And during my time in Kobe, I wrote a few articles for an expat magazine, *Kobe Times,* which led to self-publishing a booklet called *Kids in Kobe.*

At this point in my talk, I spoke about how the Universe, fate, or God sometimes offers an unexpected opportunity. And *Kids in Kobe* had provided that. Not long after publishing my booklet, a Japanese real estate agent specialising in expat rentals contacted me. Could I, he asked, draw maps for him with the landmark icons—like those in my booklet?

Long before Google Maps, navigating cities in Japan was challenging for expats. Road signs written in Japanese are difficult to memorise, and many roads don't have names. Japanese cities are divided into north, south, east, west and centre. Further subdivisions are numbered, and then most streets and the myriad of alleyways are likewise allocated a number. Confusingly, the subdivisions of Kobe are not chronological. So, at that time, expats learnt to navigate Kobe through landmarks such as the octopus bridge, Ikuta Jinja—one of Japan's oldest Shinto shrines—and the Kobe Mosque. To help readers find places I had referenced in my book, I drew maps with tiny drawings of these places—and others—on an early Mac computer. Accepting the real estate agent's offer to create maps for his properties, led me down an unexpected path.

In a small expat community, people soon hear about what others are doing. Before long, I had a trickle of orders to do simple design work. Later, when we returned to the UK, I started offering these services as desktop publishing, which wasn't yet a thing on personal computers. In time my work evolved into a fully-fledged graphic design business.

In my first year of trading, I met two wonderful human beings. One was a printer who took me under his wing and showed me how to correctly prepare artwork for printing. The other was a computer-savvy freelance designer who generously taught me how to use graphic design software. Slowly my business grew. I realised I was good at finding solutions and had lots of creative ideas that, over time, I learnt how to translate into artwork. From working alone in the box room at home, I eventually had four employees, and our final move was to a spacious, purpose-built design studio.

After eleven years of trading, my team took over the reins to look after my business while my daughters and I took time out for an unforgettable round-the-world holiday. It was during the summer and we were away for nearly seven weeks. For once there was time to simply be and think without the usual distractions. As thoughts drifted towards what I was doing with my business, I realised my work no longer excited or enchanted me. Rather, it all felt heavy. As our holiday drew to a close, I dreaded returning to work. There was no immediate option other than to do so, but this nagging feeling about my business gnawed at me.

In the autumn of that year, I found and hired Maureen, an American Life and Business Coach. Sassy, funny and direct—as I imagined all New Yorkers to be—she made me think outside of the box and asked me to consider many different options.

With Maureen's guidance, I sold my business to another design studio. Inspired by how she had helped me, I decided to follow in her footsteps and embarked on a three-year course with CoachU to become a Life Coach.

I wrapped up my talk with a quick summary. I told the women my graphic design business had been an exciting adventure until the last year of trading. And after twelve years, when it was sold, I had no regrets. Now, as a Life Coach, I said, I love what I do. The secret to success, I added, was to find work that fascinates you. Creating a business based on your passion will bring you joy.

After answering a few questions, there was a ripple of applause, and I sat down. I stayed to listen to the next speaker, and then, as the lunch break was announced, I found and thanked Amy. I was on my way out when the grey-haired woman stopped me to say thank you.

Reviewing my talk, I realised that my work journey was unusual, but why was I irritated by this woman's view that I had been lucky? Then it dawned on me. I had painted a very rosy picture. Everything I had shared was true—and I did feel fortunate. Yet, it wasn't just luck that had shaped my life. Most of all, it wasn't the whole story—not by a long shot.

I realised I hadn't spoken about the emotional turmoil of becoming a single mum when my ex-husband returned to Japan. Or the long evening hours I had worked setting up my business when my children were asleep in bed. Nor how years later, in the space of just six weeks, I lost my two biggest customers. And, of course, because it would have been totally inappropriate, I had not mentioned that I was abused as a child. Yet this unspoken part of my life has massively shaped who I am and has greatly influenced my drive and achievements in my life and work.

Once in a while, someone says something to you that stops you in your tracks. Their words might be insightful or powerful or simply an innocent comment. But because the timing is perfect, it opens a door and sets you on a new path.

The woman's comment about being lucky had this effect on me. It made me re-evaluate what I share with people. And in particular, it made me think about my story of forgiving my granddad.

Years ago, I had written my story of forgiveness, wanting to include it as a chapter in a book on finding happiness. Forgiveness and happiness may not appear to go hand-in-hand, yet happiness is often stifled when trauma is buried deep inside the psyche. Forgiving someone for inflicting pain on you is rarely easy. Yet if it can be achieved, then forgiveness allows joy to bubble up from the depths once more. I had written a handful of other chapters too, but at the time of the talk, these documents were languishing in a folder on my desktop.

The day after the talk, I decided to open these files and re-read what I had written. Was writing this book something I should do? I was still unsure. *Was it OK to share such a personal story?* Would it be easier or better to use a client's story instead? I am a private person at heart. Did I wish for everyone to know what had happened to me as a child? Would there be consequences—personally or professionally? Eventually, I realised my hang-ups about sharing were just my stuff. At this point in my life, it feels far more important to help as many people as I can on their healing journey.

It seemed that the woman who thanked me had unknowingly sent me a message from the Universe. At the time, I was still undecided about the why or how of the book, yet something inside compelled me to pick-up from where I had left off and just write.

Completing this book still took me far longer than perhaps it could or should have taken. Yet now it feels like it is the perfect time to release it into the world. My greatest wish for this book is that you will find ideas, inspiration or motivation to help you on your healing journey to find inner happiness.

Portland, October 2023.

Begin your journey to happiness

Our sorrows and wounds are healed
only when we touch them with compassion.
♥ Buddha

A swan glides serenely across the water. White feathers preened to perfection. The curve of its neck held high. It is a picture of beauty. Yet under the water, the view is very different. Large webbed feet on stumpy black legs work like pistons in a steam engine. It requires a massive amount of energy beneath the surface to make it look so easy from above.

I've met many swan-like people. From above, everything looks good. Sometimes amazingly good. Yet hidden from sight is a pool of sadness, anger, shame, or anxiety. These emotions are still there because the trauma experienced has not healed. We imagine such trauma as something terrible, horrific, or sickening. Sadly, often it is—but not always. Small traumas in childhood inflicted by an absentminded or troubled parent can also affect the adult we become. Likewise, uncomfortable, unjust or humiliating events in adulthood can dwell in the psyche long after they happen.

Under-the-surface emotions can be triggered when we are reminded of an earlier traumatic event. Then feelings about the current event are amplified by the unhealed wound. When this happens, everything feels more intense—it's scarier, sadder, or we feel angrier than expected. Feeling out of our depth with the onslaught of emotions, we push them away or try to ignore them. We might even smile and attempt to laugh it off. At these times, we may be the only one who knows just how *not OK* we are. Then, like the swan, it takes a massive amount of energy to maintain a façade of *I'm fine*, when deep inside we are not.

For a very long time, I was like a swan too. I suspect most people had no idea what was happening beneath the surface. This is perhaps why I notice other swans. I've travelled the path that many of you are on. My journey is still ongoing, but I've forgiven, healed and let go of a great deal of old emotional pain—and so can you. Being happy isn't an exclusive club that forbids entry for those who have been traumatised or who feel they don't deserve to be happy. You can change your life for the better. This opportunity is available to everyone, and I would love for you to be happier starting today.

Today?

Yes, right now, you can choose to begin your journey moving towards a happier life. This is true even if you are feeling desperately sad, angry, hurt or forlorn. Or even if you think being happy is impossible. Choice alone won't make feeling better happen. Action is needed. But never underestimate the power of choice, because this alone sets in motion a host of biological, mental and emotional changes.

What does being happy look like to you? This may seem like a strange question, and perhaps you don't have an exact answer. And that's OK for now—it will become more apparent as you discover what blocks you from being happy. For most people, happiness includes feeling loved, safe, content, at peace and having a sense of belonging, sprinkled with moments of excitement and elation. It helps, though, to move beyond generalities and define what is important to you.

Happiness comes in many flavours, like Ben and Jerry's ice creams. Mellow flavours like vanilla, represent contentment and feeling peaceful. While ice-creams with ribbon swirls, crunchy nuts and chewy bits are more akin to joy, glee, and exuberance. Often, we identify happiness as the latter, seeking it as solace when we feel sad. Then, it may feel like contentment is inferior, as if it's not enough. Yet every form of happiness is a precious experience. Consider what is needed to enjoy the quieter moments of life, as well as what makes you laugh and jump for joy.

To begin your journey, create a happiness list. Simply write or create a digital document of everything you believe would enhance your happiness. Add ideas, life events and experiences you wish to have, listing them as they occur to you. It's totally OK to add things that don't appeal to others. For example, my happy list includes sea swimming. Even in winter, when the cold makes my skin turn bright red, it feels exhilarating. It doesn't matter that many think I'm crazy for doing this! Check-in with your heart and not your head. Even if you desire something that isn't immediately possible, still make a note of it.

Seeking happiness doesn't exclude other emotions. Rather every emotion has a role to play in our lives. However, when happiness is a regular companion in life, it becomes easier to deal with any troubling emotions, and these are less likely to get stuck in the psyche.

William Arthur Ward, an American motivational writer, coined the phrase *Happiness is an inside job*. And when I speak of inner happiness, this is the same principle. People in our lives and events may influence our happiness, but they can't make us happy or feel anything unless we give them permission to do so. Your inner happiness is a choice—even though it may not feel like that's the case.

There are vast numbers of people in the world today on their healing journey—many are a long way down the line. So, know that in choosing to heal your trauma and to enhance your happiness, you are not alone. We don't always hear of their healing stories because, so often, it's too hard to share.

Many who have done a lot of work on themselves quietly get on with their lives. Even when things are tough, they seem to walk through life more easily, with a quick smile and a kind word for others. Their journey and your journey will not be the same, and it may not always be easy. Yet, the gift of compassion for others and inner peace are worthy rewards for doing this work.

In the beginning, it can be hard to talk about or consider the impact of hurt, anger, shame and grief or any ugliness in life. It's more comfortable to shy away and pretend everything is OK. We all wish for a magic wand at times because the reality of dealing with what happened to you can be scary. And yet, being brave enough to explore the dark eddies of life surprisingly shows us how to find our light, which ultimately makes us feel better.

Unhealed trauma—and we all have some—dampens our ability to be joyful, curious and live life with zest. By choosing to heal, being gentle with yourself, you can figure it out. Your future does not need to be defined by your past, no matter how horrible it was. You too, can walk through life more easily.

In the following chapters, you will find healing stories, tips, ideas, suggestions and exercises to help you. The exercises have been road-tested with my clients over many years and will help you see things differently as well as ease areas where you are stuck. A few may not be relevant to your personal circumstances, so skip these. Trust your judgement as to which exercises will help you the most—but actively choose to do some of them! These are also best done when you reach them in the book.

So, are you ready to swim in the depths for a while? To discover how to let go and find your inner happiness?

Let's dive in and begin.

My story:
Forgiving Granddad

Ever since happiness heard your name,
it has been running through the streets trying to find you.
♥ Hafez

Before I began my healing journey, I would tell people I had a wonderful childhood. And mostly, that's true—I did. And yet, as a child, I was also sexually abused by my granddad.

This paradox of being happy as a child and yet dealing with such distressing events is more common than might be imagined. Some of my clients who survived childhood abuse likewise paint a delightful picture of their early years. And even when the rays of sunshine seem few and far between, most people still desire to portray a happy childhood. It is what we had hoped for and wanted.

Those of us who were neglected, harmed or traumatised as youngsters are like the swans. We strived or still aim for perfection as we swim, yet under the surface, it's often not so pretty. We hide the truth because we wish to divert prying eyes from the shame, anguish or anger that is felt. Telling someone the truth is risky because you can never tell how someone will react to such a revelation. The fear of being judged or abandoned is scary. It's easier for the messy, complicated and sometimes horrific to stay hidden from view.

Every story of childhood abuse is unique, yet within these stories, there are common threads. I hope that telling my story and how I forgave my granddad may inspire you to consider forgiving anyone who has hurt, harmed or caused you pain.

I grew up in a small town in Leicestershire. Its working-class status was looked down upon by the posher, prettier neighbouring town. My mum's family owned a butcher's shop, and they were financially well off. My dad came from a poorer family who had moved many times. Dad attended six different schools and left in his early teens, but he was naturally clever and very ambitious.

Not long after I arrived into the world, Dad, with the help of Mum, started an electrical contracting business. In the beginning, Dad used Mum's scooter to get from one job to another. He would stuff his tools into a jacket pocket and place a drum of cable on one arm.

When I was three, maybe four, Mum and Dad bought a terraced house above a small shop. Soon the large window facing the street was filled with light fittings and all kinds of electrical bits and bobs. Mum took care of the shop between looking after my sister and me. In the back garden, Dad built a large workshop and a small office. Soon a handful of electricians and apprentices were working for Dad, and my youngest sister joined our family.

As was common in the 1960s, shops were closed every Wednesday afternoon, and we would visit Big Grandma's—my mum's mum—for afternoon tea. She wasn't particularly big; my sisters and I bestowed this name on her to distinguish her from Small Grandma, who was tiny. In the kitchen at Big Grandma's was a large table which was pushed into the corner. There, affixed to the wall was padded seating, a bit like that found in restaurants of that time. The table was easily large enough for us all to sit together. I loved Big Grandma's teas. Instead of being given a plate of food as happened at home, we chose what we wished to eat. The table was spread with all kinds of delicious food. A home-cooked ham was often there, along with a choice of sandwiches, some tinned salmon and always slices of cucumber and onion soaked in vinegar. To finish our tea, there would be thick slices of Angel or Battenberg cake.

We didn't visit Small Grandma's so often, and I don't remember having meals there. My earliest memory of Granddad—my dad's dad—was at a family gathering at their house. We were in the back room. I was sitting straddled on one of Grandad's knees. He sang a nursery rhyme to me as he jiggled me up and down. Hidden by my dress, he had placed his hand underneath me. His fingers made the jiggling uncomfortable, but more than that, I didn't like that he was singing a baby song to me.

By the time I was seven, Mum and Dad's business was doing well. With more money available, they paid for my pony riding lessons. I was perhaps eight when Dad bought a Dartmoor pony—Brandy—from a horse auction. I am reasonably sure it was Mum's desire to see me and my sisters learn to ride as she had done, rather than us begging her to have a pony. But we all fell in love with Brandy. Over the next few years, ponies Misty, Tarquin and a donkey called Big Ears became part of our family. My sisters and I rode our ponies, learnt how to groom and muck out, and took part in gymkhanas during the summer months.

It was also around this time that my friend and I began going to the local swimming pool—baths as they were called back then—without our parents. There we regularly talked to a man who arrived in a wheelchair. A lifeguard helped him into the pool. His legs were withered, but he had a powerful chest and strong arms, and he was usually the fastest swimmer in the pool. I don't remember his name—or even that of the girl who came with me—but he kindly taught us both to swim. In the water, I lost my clumsiness and felt graceful, as I'm sure the disabled man did too.

When I turned nine, I began pestering my parents to join the local swimming club. Initially, Mum and Dad were hesitant, but they relented, and soon my sister and I were attending training sessions. Later still, my youngest sister joined us. Dad, in time, became the swimming club's president and Mum the club secretary—even though neither were strong swimmers.

I was nine years old when Granddad asked my parents if I could help him prepare his garden produce. I'm not sure, but I think the visits were weekly. I know my parents regularly took me to his house. They were completely unaware that Granddad had other plans for me beyond helping in the garden.

My grandparents' house had a large back garden, most of which was a vegetable plot. At the far end, there were two large greenhouses, a small tool shed and a garage. One of the greenhouses was crammed with tomato plants, and vegetable seedlings. The other one was used for growing pink carnations and red geraniums. The sweet smell of ripening tomatoes and the strange perfume of geraniums still reminds me of that time.

Each visit began with gardening tasks such as weeding, potting seedlings, digging up potatoes, picking tomatoes and other seasonal vegetables. We placed the produce in brown paper bags. Sometimes Granddad would take me with him in his car to sell these to a nearby caravan park. More often, Granddad would leave the bags on the greenhouse shelf for delivery after I went home.

After our time in the garden, Granddad would ask me to go with him into the garage. He closed the two wood doors, and the light was now dim as it came through the grimy window. He would unlock and open the two back doors of his pale blue Morris Traveller, which was like a small van with windows at the sides. Inside, Granddad had already spread a blanket on the flat floor. My memories of what happened on those occasions are hazy. He used to lie on top of me. I could feel his fingers touch me, but one day I realised it wasn't his fingers rubbing against me anymore because I saw his hands on either side of me. Afterwards, we went to the kitchen, and Small Grandma would give me a glass of lemonade with a biscuit.

I have no recall of the first time Granddad asked me to lie down for him or how many months it continued. I know he took me at least once to his shed on the allotment. I also have a vague memory of lying on the potting greenhouse's creaky, wide-bottom shelf.

The memory that is the clearest is the day Grandma had gone out for the day. Instead of leading me to the garage, Granddad took me into the front room—Grandma's pride and joy. Granddad, in his navy work dungarees, his hair ruffled from his wide-brimmed hat, and soil under his fingernails looked out of place in this room reserved for best. Grandma's pretty ornaments sitting on the mantelpiece were not, she had admonished on an earlier visit, to be played with. These were precious, she said, and I might break them. Granddad asked me to lie down on the floor. The carpet was softer than the blanket in the car. My white panties were removed, and Granddad, still fully dressed but with his button flies open, laid down on top of me. I looked up at the precious ornaments and wished that I too could not be touched. Granddad's weight was crushing me so much I thought I might break. He brought his face closer to mine. One of his prominent fleshy ear lobes brushed across my face as he whispered,

'You'll start to like it when you're ten.'

Maybe it was pure fear that kept this memory alive. I didn't want to like what Granddad did to me—I hated it, and increasingly I hated Granddad too. I wanted him to stop asking me to lie down for him, but I didn't know how, and I was too scared to tell Mum or Dad.

Granddad repeatedly told me how much he loved me. He said that if you love someone you lie down for them. Then almost in the same breath he told me that if I spoke to anyone about the things we did, I would be taken away from Mum and Dad. At the end of every visit, I had to promise not to share our special secret.

Then came a day when Mum asked me about what I did when I went to see Granddad. I don't remember much of what she asked or what I said.

Much later, I found out that it was my aunt who had raised the alarm. She had been sexually abused by her father—my granddad—too.

What I remember the most is begging Mum to never let me see Granddad again. And, apart from two chance encounters many years later, he was, from then on, absent from my life.

Granddad was punished by being shut out of our family, but the abuse was never reported to the police. Without any visible signs of punishment, and in the way children often do, I thought I must have done something wrong. So, I vowed to be very good—then, it couldn't happen again. It sounds so innocent, but making such a pledge can warp your life.

Although I didn't know until I was in my thirties, Mum had sought advice from our doctor about as how to deal with what happened to me. He recommended that she didn't mention it to me again. He said in time I would forget about it. Hearing this as an adult was incredibly hard to process. *How and why did he think that? How could Mum have followed such terrible advice?* Yet Mum always revered doctors. Earlier in her life she had trained to be a nurse. Back then, doctors were considered to be superior beings, and their instructions were beyond question. So, Mum told Dad not to talk to me about it either. Apart from no longer visiting my paternal grandparents, everyone pretended nothing had happened.

But I didn't forget. Even though there are gaps in my memory, especially the finer details, I have always known what Granddad did to me.

In my early teens, my first relationships with boys were, not unsurprisingly, complicated. Mostly I suspect it was typical teenager stuff, but several boys accused me of being a tease who then slammed on the brakes.

Wanting to be a good person—like the swan—I strove for perfection. I worked hard at school, swam with the swimming club, and played netball and hockey for the school teams. I also rode and helped to look after our ponies. I have no idea how I crammed so much into my life.

My high school headmistress, though, was not impressed. Instead, to her, I was a nuisance. Weekly I would go to her office to reclaim things I'd lost. On several occasions, she came to our classroom, dangling one of my belongings in the air. *Who has lost this?* she asked rhetorically knowing full well it was mine. Out of despair, Mum had labelled all of my bags, books and PE kit, hoping items I lost would be found. Perhaps my headmistress thought humiliation would cure my absentmindedness. If that was her intention, it didn't work—it simply brought up intense dislike for her. And, although I'm not sure, I suspect some of my forgetfulness was also down to dissociative moments.

For many children trying to cope with abusive behaviour, a protective mechanism called dissociation kicks in. Although I didn't know it at the time—in fact, not until decades later—I know that I dissociated too. This happens when the psyche can't cope with the overwhelming torrent of emotions. It's an automatic response that disconnects and separates the mind from current consciousness. Becoming numb to what is happening or has happened makes it easier to deal with. Dissociation can also bury events so deeply that much of the pain and the memories are inaccessible by the conscious mind. This allows children to separate the scary stuff from what is good, OK or at least tolerable.

Statistics show that ninety per cent of abusers are known to the child, and sadly, so many of these are family members. So, mixed in with the neglect, harm and abuse, there are also times when the perpetrator is kind and loving. For a child, these confusing patterns of behaviour make the awful stuff even harder to process.

In its mild form, most of us have dissociated at one time or another. Like when we realise we have no recollection of what we have just read. Or when we drive home on automatic pilot. Or when we are so absorbed in drawing, cooking or tinkering with a car that we completely lose track of time. Dissociation like this, lasts for moments or minutes, but in severe cases, it can last for hours or even days, which is disorientating and can lead to mental health disorders.

For me, memories from when I was eight to ten are sparse and distant. When I try to recapture elements of my life from this time—like trying to remember the names of my teachers and classmates—it's like trying to catch fragments of a dream. It feels like my mind swept away good, bad and indifferent memories from this time to help me to stay safe.

I now know I can easily dissociate. I sense this happened regularly in my early teenage years, much to my headmistress and Mum's frustration. They were perplexed as to why I so frequently lost belongings. I didn't get it either. I tried hard to stop this habit as I intensely disliked being called absent-minded.

For those trying to piece together partial memories, it can also feel like the events didn't happen to them. Rather, it feels more like knowing what happened to a best friend. In this way, the emotions that arose are distant and beyond being felt.

So, when in my early twenties I met my husband-to-be, I told him my childhood was great. At that time, the abuse seemed unimportant. In the twelve years we were together, it simply didn't occur to me to tell him or anyone else what had happened to me as a child.

Overall, the early years with my husband were good ones. Being in a stable relationship and the arrival of our daughters was very healing for me. But cracks in our marriage began to show while we were in Singapore. By the time we landed in Japan, it felt like the way we viewed the world and what we wanted from life was irreconcilably different. We tried hard to make our marriage work, yet it was less than great. We decided to return to the UK to see if we could get things back on track, but instead of making things better, our disagreements—we rarely had full-on arguments—became worse. We were both miserable. In the spring of 1990, we mutually agreed to go our separate ways, and my husband returned to Japan.

In the months after he left, I thought I was OK. In many ways, it was a relief to no longer pretend that we were happy. However, I had begun to have terrible nightmares. Some of these were about my husband, but most were about my eldest daughter, who in the dream-world, was always in danger. In these nightmares, I was never fast enough or near enough to save her. I'd wake up feeling terrified, with my heart racing faster than it ever did when I used to take part in running races in Japan.

One night, after kissing my young daughters goodnight, I walked down the stairs, sat on the last step and silently wept. I felt lost and alone. I felt like a failure for not making my marriage work. We were in a town in Oxfordshire, chosen to help my husband commute to London, but to me, it was an ugly place. My closest friends were scattered across the globe. My family were unaware of my pain, and I didn't feel I could tell them either. Added to this, I often felt out of my depth with my new business—at times feeling like a fraud, as I had no training. But I had never cried before. I was the strong one. When things were tough, I always put a positive spin on it and found a way to move forward. Yet this pool of un-cried tears kept welling up inside of me. This time I was drowning in a sorrow so deep I felt that it might be easier to die than to go on. Finally, I realised I needed help.

My first counsellor was a large, quiet man with grey hair and deep blue eyes. He wore a corduroy jacket and crumpled trousers. Although I can picture him in my mind's eye, I don't remember his name. He sat very still as he listened to me speak about my marriage falling apart and my nightmares. He asked me to start a dream journal. In our early sessions, we looked at what my dreams might mean. I began to see those about not saving my daughter were really about me as a child not being saved. What had happened to me, my counsellor had asked, when I was my daughter's age? With lots of encouragement, for the first time, I began to speak about Granddad.

I cried so much in those sessions—perhaps catching up on all the years that I hadn't allowed myself to do so—and slowly, I began to see the hidden impact of the abuse. Even not arguing with my husband—trying always to be good—were, in part, down to what had happened.

In our sessions, I learnt that childhood abuse was common and that its darkness casts a shadow over a life long after the abuse has ended. This new knowledge lifted a massive weight off my shoulders. Now it seems naive that I didn't know this back then.

The hourly sessions with my counsellor helped me see life differently. Without consciously searching, I stumbled across several books about sexual abuse. Even at the time, it struck me as odd that I had not looked for books on this subject before. Survivors' accounts brought yet more tears to my eyes, for their words were mine. We shared hidden, harrowing shame and guilt that wasn't ours to hold. Their nightmares of terror were similar to mine. Their healing allowed me to look at the part of my soul that had not been given permission to speak.

Then after almost a year of deep introspection, I abruptly told my counsellor that my healing was complete. I saw and felt sadness in his eyes as I thanked him, but I was impatient to get on with my life. I wanted my life to be perfect again—I was tired of digging up the past. Even though I now see this may have prolonged my healing, it's hard not to admire my younger self's determination to make everything OK. The trouble is once you have let the genie out of the bottle it doesn't so easily go back inside.

There were several short spells working with a psychotherapist and several other counsellors in the years that followed. In those sessions, I dove once more into the depths to further understand and heal the abuse. And I still carefully hid all that was going on under the surface from the outside world. However, each time I went through the process, I healed a little more. Yet there was always a day when I suddenly finished these sessions too. The slightest improvement was enough for me to believe that I didn't need any more help.

The years passed by, and I pushed forward in life with my lovely daughters and my graphic design business. The latter was growing and making a good name for itself. I liked the challenge of finding creative solutions for my customers and leading my small team of employees. There were moments when I caught myself being absent, but I dismissed it, telling myself everyone had these moments.

In the autumn of 2001, my eldest daughter would go to university, and my youngest daughter would start her course at a local college. To celebrate these milestones, we took the summer off and travelled around the world. We visited Jakarta, Singapore and Kobe followed by an overland adventure across the USA, including a week white water rafting through the Grand Canyon.

In the last few days of our amazing holiday, we all longed to once more sleep in our own beds. But something had shifted inside of me. Work felt like walking through treacle, and irrationally, I didn't want to do it anymore. I was excited for my daughters beginning their new life chapters, yet the nest was feeling empty. Now that our holiday was over, I wanted to find a life partner, but that too felt impossible. As was my habit, I didn't share much of how I felt with family and friends. It seemed ungrateful even to mention it—but my closest friend diagnosed it as post-holiday blues. She said it wasn't surprising that I felt the way I did. After such a fantastic adventure, everyday life would feel mundane by comparison. I knew she was right—at least partially—but instinctively, I knew there was something else going on.

That's when I began working with Maureen. As well as coaching me through options for my business, which was my biggest concern, she gently probed into what else might be bothering me. We spoke a little about

Granddad, but I was hesitant. *Did I really need to revisit it again?* Maureen didn't push this any further, instead she suggested that I read *The Journey* by Brandon Bays, which I did.

Brandon's book begins with the discovery that she had a pelvic tumour the size of a basketball. Frightened by her doctor's recommendation for immediate surgery, Brandon begged to delay the surgery by 30-days. At that time, Brandon was a healer, and she asked for this time to attempt healing her body naturally.

Her doctor did not believe in such possibilities but reluctantly agreed to Brandon's request. Brandon tried everything she knew. Her already healthy diet became supercharged, and she sought the help of other healers. Yet her most significant breakthrough came from a weekend spent alone, working with her emotions. Brandon allowed herself to feel all of the pain and hurt she had hidden for so long. Then, weeping for all that had been lost, she felt her body respond. After the allotted 30-days had passed, much to the surprise of her sceptical doctor, her tumour had shrunk to the size of a tennis ball. Not long after that, the tumour completely disappeared.

Brandon's book concluded with how she had trained other therapists to do what has become known as Journey Therapy.

I was intrigued. Brandon's approach was different from what I had experienced in counselling and psychotherapy. On her website, I found a list of Journey Therapists. I saw one of them was Joel Young, who also lived in Oxfordshire. Following instinct more than anything else, I called him and booked a three-hour healing session at his home.

I liked Joel instantly. He had a calm presence with a soft and frequent smile. He led the way up a creaky wood staircase into his attic therapy room. Sparsely decorated with just two comfy chairs, it nonetheless felt cosy. As we settled into the session, Joel asked me to tell him what I needed help with. So, I told him I thought I was still holding on to old emotions from childhood abuse, even though it didn't rationally make sense to me.

I don't remember much of what was said in the first part of our session. I vaguely recall Joel leading me through a Journey process. However, I vividly remember that towards the end of our session Joel asked me to forgive Granddad.

I was stunned and even angry at the suggestion. *He was the adult, and I was just nine when it happened. I had not done anything wrong: no way was I going to forgive him!* Wisely, Joel didn't push it. Instead, he asked me what I wanted to do about my granddad.

With absolutely no forgiveness in my heart, I asked Joel if I could kick his soul as far away from me as I could. Joel nodded his permission. In my mind's eye, I watched Granddad's soul strangely appear like a ball before soaring high into the sky. It became smaller and smaller, travelling further and further away until it reached the outer edge of the Milky Way. Even though he had died years before this healing session, the thought of Granddad's soul being in a place where he could no longer hurt me made me feel safe. I was aware of how illogical and embarrassingly child-like this was. Granddad was long gone—how could he still hurt me? Nonetheless, this new feeling of being safe swept through me, and I felt I could now truly move forward.

At the end of 2002, I sold my graphic design business, and I trained to become a Life and Business Coach. The process changed my life. Curiosity led me down unexpected paths, guiding me to talks and workshops. Teachers, gurus and experts in the world of self-development challenged my beliefs about God, the Universe and how the world worked. Slowly, I realigned my beliefs, shed my old, agnostic skin, and my new spiritual-self blossomed.

By the end of 2005, my coaching practice was thriving. I was helping people create better and happier lives, and I loved my new work. In my personal life, though, there were gremlins that niggled away at my happiness. A Life Coach's mantra is, *walk your talk*, and I was aware that I wasn't in integrity. I realised I needed to do more healing and find a way to forgive Granddad.

I reached out once more to Joel, and we arranged to meet. Early on the allotted day, Joel welcomed me into his new home. The intervening years since we last met had been kind to Joel—he looked even more at peace than before. Dressed in loose-fitting white trousers and a matching grandfather-style shirt, Joel led me into the lounge, and I sat in a comfy chair. I noticed his collection of large crystals and the scent of incense burning. Large floor to ceiling windows revealed a vista of meadowland with a meandering river. It was a beautiful, peaceful place.

And then I was suddenly filled with doubt. How on earth I was going to forgive my granddad for all that he had done? Half of me wanted to tell Joel this was a big mistake and that I needed to leave. But instead, I took a deep breath to ground myself and asked,

'Why do I need to forgive my granddad, Joel?'

'Because you need to forgive yourself.'

I was surprised by his reply and thought, *but I didn't do anything wrong*.

Joel, noticing I was lost in thought, gave me some more space before adding, 'You haven't let go of your granddad yet. And in all of this, not intentionally, of course, you too have played a role in this.'

I sat for a while. Tears rolled down my cheeks. Not again. I didn't want to cry again. What was *my role* supposed to mean? I reached for the tissues and tried to think. Still, no words came. Joel saw I was struggling.

Caringly, he said: 'It's not about condoning your granddad's behaviour. What he did was utterly wrong.'

More silence. Inside my head, my thoughts were clamouring, *Why was this so goddamn hard? Why am I still allowing him to impact my life 40 years on?*

Memories of lying in the back of the Morris Traveller flooded my mind as another part of me tried to shut them down.

Joel's voice broke through the silence.

'Tell me what your granddad was like.'

What was he like? I hated him so much that I had not considered what he was like as a person. I hadn't spoken to him since I was nine, and no one in our family spoke of him either. Thoughts whirled through my mind, not making much sense.

I came back into the room with a jolt to see that Joel was still patiently waiting. Good healers are comfortable with silence—they know how this gives precious space to sort things out internally.

Haltingly, I told Joel that Granddad loved gardening, and that he was proud of his tomatoes, especially how they smelt and how sweet they tasted with a pinch of salt. And I suddenly realised that my love of gardening came from him.

Joel changed tack. He asked me if there had been other abuse within my family. I shared that I wasn't the only one caught in this tangled web. My aunt had been abused too. I told Joel that my aunt had recently told me more of her story. She told me that when she was fourteen, she told her mum—Small Grandma—what Granddad was doing, but she wasn't believed. Considering Joel's question, I silently wondered if there had been others.

Joel told me that abuse often travels through many generations. There was a strong likelihood that someone had abused my granddad when he was a child—possibly a family member who had also been abused, and so on.

Joel then calmly asked, 'Did you know it was wrong at the time?'

I could see he was asking me to step out of my emotional stuckness—to look at what had happened as a fully conscious adult. *At nine years old, did I know it was wrong?* Shame flushed my cheeks.

'Yes, I think I did.'

More memories and confusion flooded in. Innocently, I once asked Granddad, 'Are you trying to make a baby with me?'

I had seen our pet dog Cindy being mated and the resulting puppies. By nine, I had figured that much out.

Joel gently asked, 'If you knew it was wrong, why didn't you speak out?'

Like a truculent child, I replied: 'I was nine! He shouldn't have done those terrible things to me!'

Instantly, I saw I was stepping into the role of a victim, blaming Granddad, but I still couldn't get my head around this. I didn't want it to be anything other than he was a monster and I was a helpless little girl.

Then up bubbled out of me, 'I was too scared to tell, in case what Granddad said was true and I would be taken away from my mum and dad.'

Joel calmly agreed, 'Your granddad was the adult. What he did to you was so very wrong. When you were nine, you knew this, but it was too scary to tell anyone.' He continued, 'Is it possible that not forgiving your granddad is connected to not wanting to forgive the little girl who did her best to survive in a truly horrible situation? Are you judging and blaming her for not having said anything?'

More tears. I was beginning to see just how much I had not forgiven my scared, nine-year-old self.

As the hours passed, Joel repeatedly reassured me that my younger self had done nothing wrong. In the circumstances, she had been courageous. We went over my old stories again. This time with new, compassionate eyes, I finally saw Granddad as a weak and sick man who may also have been abused. With compassion rising within me, I mentally looked him in the eye and forgave him, and this time his soul drifted away from me in peace, no longer tied to me.

Today there is no resentment or hatred in my soul towards Granddad or about what happened to me. It was awful, but the love of my family helped to balance it out.

My intuitive abilities awakened during that time. No longer trusting the words of adults, I sought to know a deeper truth by checking in with what

I sensed and felt. This ability to read people and situations is a gift and invaluable in my work. I also believe my journey makes it easier for me to help others navigate their rivers of pain. I feel blessed to do the work I do, and I probably do it better because of what happened to me as a child.

Become emotionally savvy

It would be impossible to estimate how much time and energy we invest in trying to fix, change and deny our emotions—especially the ones that shake us at our very core, like hurt, jealousy, loneliness, shame, rage and grief.
♥ Debbie Ford

Navigating the world post-trauma is rarely straightforward because things taken for granted before may no longer make sense. Like who to trust. Any inkling that truth is not being spoken or something is amiss leads to sensing whether or not it is safe. This sensing is done by tapping into our intuitive knowing, which tells us if we need to steer clear of a drunk parent or partner. Or refrain from saying what is in our heart. Or if we can trust someone with a secret.

Survivors are frequently highly intuitive. This makes sense when you know that most intuitive messages are connected to fear, whose role is to protect us from harm. When fear is free-flowing, we are more intuitive. Sometimes after trauma, fear can get stuck. Without intuition to guide us, everything can seem fearful, which leads to excessive worry, anxiety and even moments of panic.

All emotions have a place in our life—even those we shy away from, like shame, rage and jealousy. Emotions are messages that provide insights into our life and what is happening in the world. When happiness bubbles up from within, we instantly recognise the message that life is good. So, we smile, laugh and play. By emoting these feelings, we enjoy them, and then they dissipate. When emotions complete their process in this way, they naturally flow through us. Yet those that take us to a scary place or feel distressing are not so easy to deal with or emote. When we cannot process or deal with the complexity of feelings, moods and thoughts, we push them away, or force them back inside. Emotions that don't flow, even if slowly as in grief, negatively affect our happiness, well-being and health.

Becoming happier isn't about shunning or suppressing these challenging emotions. Rather, becoming emotionally savvy means we can discover new and healthier ways of processing them. With greater emotional expertise, we become more adept at handling what arises from within, which massively improves the quality of our relationships.

AN EMOTIONAL JOURNEY FROM TURIN TO TOKYO TO TIMBUKTU

Imagine you are in the Italian city of Turin, sitting at a table in a restaurant. While you wait for your meal to arrive, you do some people-watching. A family of six are sitting around the next table. There looks to be a mum and dad, with a son with his wife, another woman—perhaps a daughter—and a boy who looks to be in his early teens. Their food arrives, and the mum begins passing around the big plates of fish, vegetables and pasta. When she encourages her son to have more vegetables, he laughingly protests, *No, Mamma*, placing his hand over his plate. Before they start to eat, the dad turns to his wife, placing a hand on her shoulder. It appears she knows what he is about to say, as she smiles then half covers her face with her hands. The dad then regales his family with some tale that ends with his free arm spread wide and a big grin. Everyone laughs before picking up their cutlery and beginning to eat. Was it a family joke? Perhaps. Even without comprehending much of what you heard, you know they are all happy.

Now, in your mind's eye, transport yourself to Shinjuku, in Tokyo, to a place tourists call Godzilla Street. Each side of this short road has ten-story buildings adorned with neon signs that make Piccadilly Circus look tame by comparison. In this busy street, the cacophony of sounds and the kaleidoscope of colours is disorientating. On the street are restaurants, convenience stores, newsagents, a huge Imax cinema and a train station entrance. At the end of the street is Hotel Gracery, with its distinctive, narrow thirty-story tower block that looks like a gigantic barcode. Up on the tenth floor is an enormous model of Godzilla peering over the edge and looking down on the entrance, as if guarding it.

Under Godzilla's scrutiny, two business-suited Japanese men stand face to face. Even in this crowded environment the men's voices can be heard above the background sounds.

The eyes of the man facing you are darting around, looking for an escape route. The man whose face you cannot see clenches his fist and is now yelling. Despite not understanding a single word, you know one man is angry and the other is scared. Sensing danger, you move away from these men.

Now, mentally whisk yourself to Timbuktu, deep in the heart of central Africa. This tiny city in Mali was once a place of learning and rich from gold mining. Now it is a poor place, with desert sands encroaching on abandoned houses. In the city centre stands an impressive university mosque, the stature of which once matched the Oxford Colleges. Tall walls surround an inner building. The structure is built with mud bricks, plastered to create surreal shapes, and finished with a sprinkling of yellow sand. A handful of people are walking by on the dusty road outside the walls. One woman catches your eye. She is wearing a colourful traditional dress with a pale blue scarf covering her hair. She is walking slowly. You notice her face looks puffy. She raises a hand to her face as if she might be wiping tears from her eyes. You don't know her circumstances, but you sense she is sad, and you wonder if you can help her.

Eight billion human beings live on planet Earth—and we're all unique. Collectively, we communicate in over 7,000 languages. However, few of us speak more than one or two languages beyond our native tongue. Yet everyone on the planet has a communication channel that we all understand—the language of our emotions.

DIVING DEEP INTO THE EMOTIONS

What exactly are emotions? Do they begin as electro-chemical changes in the body that we interpret as feelings? Or do instinctive reactions create feelings which trigger changes to our body chemistry? Scientists are still looking for more jigsaw puzzle pieces to answer these questions. Meanwhile, neurologists, psychologists, doctors and those who study behaviour don't yet agree on how to define emotions. Most dictionaries sidestep the issue too, stating; *Emotions are strong feelings such as joy, anger or sadness.* Their definition begs the question, are emotions and feelings the same thing? Or are feelings the result of becoming conscious of an emotion?

The following is far from complete, but it gets closer to my definition of emotions:

* Emotions are complex experiences that are not always easy to describe to others.
* All forms of social interactions and life events can trigger an emotional response.
* Emotions are experienced as feelings and bodily sensations which may result in changes in our behaviour and mood.
* Not a day passes without the expression of many emotions—most play out in the background of our life, but some days, they are full-on.

From the moment we are born, we experience emotions, which provide information about what is going on within us. We know they are more than thoughts because we can think about emotions yet not *feel* them. We also witness emotional reactions in others, which may influence our feelings. We may later mimic their behaviour if we perceive there are benefits in doing so. Like, how a young child learns that crocodile tears and a pout may get their parents to give them what they desire.

Bodily responses to emotions range from irrepressible smiles when we feel joyous to the hairs on the back of our neck prickling when we are fearful, to butterflies in our tummy when we are excited. Somewhere within our understanding there is a sense that emotions convey messages from our subconscious into consciousness.

We have hundreds of names to describe our emotions and feelings, yet it can still be hard to give a name to what we are experiencing. There are also confusing, unwritten rules about what is and what is not acceptable about emotional expression. For example, it is OK to be tearful and grief-stricken for a few weeks after the death of someone we loved but not for months afterwards, especially not in the workplace. Anger might be permissible when fighting injustice, but it's considered bad in almost every other circumstance. For women, it is less acceptable to express anger than it is for men, and a man is often considered weak if he cries. With such illogical restrictions, it's no wonder we struggle to get a handle on our emotions.

One way we read emotions in others is through their facial expressions. The smile and frown are obvious, yet it is fleeting micro-expressions that cross a face which are far more telling. Our subconscious is instantly aware of these signals, influencing our reactions, especially if the micro-expression is threatening.

Most people can't fake facial expressions to convey emotions convincingly without training in acting. Like a fake smile. Natural smiles are different from those consciously created. Genuine smiles light up the eyes—probably due to body chemistry changes.

When someone is angry, their facial expressions, body posture and tone of voice are dead giveaways as to their feelings. Yet many people learn to mask anger—like an employee who wants to say *no* to their boss as it crosses a personal boundary—but still nods yes. Later, the desire to say *no* is still strong, but the brakes remain on for fear of adverse consequences. Masking anger doesn't switch off the body's chemical signals or make the anger go away. So, the angry feelings rattle around inside until they seep out in other hurtful ways or explode. Dumping anger—especially if it lands on a loved one—usually brings up shame and guilt, adding more fuel to being angry with the boss.

Happy emotions are the easiest to spot in others, showing up with smiles, quick and easy laughter, and playfulness in vocal energy. When we are happy, our brain produces more dopamine—the feel-good neurotransmitter—which gives us a surge of well-being. This change in our brain's chemistry boosts our energy, and we want to do more and share our good feelings with others.

Most people define emotions as good/bad or negative/positive. Anger is often labelled as one of the bad guys, but like all emotions, it has a rightful place in our lives. The face of anger we see most often is aggression used to manipulate, scare or threaten others. However, when we channel anger, it has a protective, healing energy. Some people like the power anger gives them over others and adopt it as a personality trait. However, abusing anger in this way will never lead to a happy life.

SEE YOUR EMOTIONS AT PLAY

Cast your mind back and recall a time when you felt joyful. Recall it with as much detail as you can. Where were you at the time? What were you doing? What was happening on this day? Now consider how long you felt joyous. Not contented or happy, which you may have experienced before or afterwards—but joyful. A few minutes? Probably. Pure joy doesn't last long, yet the beautiful sensation of inner peace, well-being and happiness that joy contains still makes it magical when it happens.

Sometimes feeling joyful feels so good that we hold on to it rather than letting it flow. Doing this changes joy into a strange energy. Laughter no longer bubbles up in gentle waves; instead, it becomes strident. Eyes lose their sparkle, and talking becomes over-animated. Forced joy is usually a coping mechanism to mask sadness, vulnerability or pain.

Now take a moment to recall a time when you felt intensely angry. Remember what happened, who said and did what to whom and the outcome. Was anger handled in an honourable way—or unleashed in an unbecoming outpouring? Or was it pushed back inside?

When anger has been expressed, even when horribly handled, it doesn't last long—at least not in its original state. Pushing anger back inside may help you keep your dignity, but its fiery energy will ultimately find a way of coming back up.

NAMING OUR EMOTIONS

Emotions are rarely single entities of experience, so we may feel annoyed, sad and embarrassed in the same moment. And some emotional states, such as grief, contain a myriad of different feelings. However, having a name for challenging emotions is often helpful. For example, realising we are not just angry, but seething. Recognising the depth of our emotional responses helps us see this can't simply be ignored or brushed under the carpet. The table overleaf lists key emotional and feeling states that are challenging to deal with. Take a moment to read down each column.

SAD	ANGER	FEAR	SHAME/GUILT	ENVY/JEALOUSY
Feeling blue	Irritated	Uneasy	Bashful	Insecure
Subdued	Annoyed	Cautious	Self-conscious	Vulnerable
Forlorn	Cross	Alarmed	Flustered	Desirous
Melancholy	Frustrated	Apprehensive	Embarrassed	Covetous
Sad	Angry	Nervous	Guilty	Envious
Weepy	Exasperated	Afraid	Ashamed	Jealous
Miserable	Furious	Fearful	Humiliated	Possessive
Depressed	Incensed	Worried	Belittled	
Despairing	Bitter	Anxious	Disgraced	**APATHY**
Anguished	Livid	Jumpy	Mortified	Bored
Maudlin	Seething	Frightened		Indifferent
Heartbroken	Vindictive	Scared		Cold
Grieving	Raging	Panicky		Apathetic
Wretched	Apoplectic	Terrified		Overwhelmed
Inconsolable	Red Mist	Petrified		Worthless

As you read down each column, do you get a sense of how the energy intensifies as you reach the bottom of the list? Also, that anger and fear energetically escalate, while the sad emotions lose their vibrance as they spiral downwards?

Recognising these shifts in energy allows you to have some conscious control over what you are feeling. For example, it is possible to nudge a feeling down to a lesser state of intensity, like consciously choosing to lessen exasperation to feeling cross. Or diminishing worry to feeling apprehensive.

How does this help? The stronger the emotion, the more energy it drains out of you, and there is less access to rational thought to find solutions. Making such shifts begins with choice. Begin by ask yourself whether these powerful feelings are serving you. If you are angry or furious with a workmate, does furious serve you more than being angry? Can you still deal with what is going on without the extra emotional energy? When an emotion's energy is lowered, we can find thought-about responses rather than knee-jerk reactions.

All emotions are designed to flow. Of the challenging emotions, pure anger can take over our mind and body in an instant. Using the tools in this book, you can learn how to lessen it quickly. Fear can stick around long after the event that triggered these feelings, which may lead to on-going anxiety, but this too can be tackled. Sadness and grief by their nature are slow moving emotions, but gently these can move forward with more purpose when they are fully understood. The tools for doing this are covered in the following chapters. With a greater understanding of our emotions, together with new ways to process them, we will be able to navigate life's difficult times more easily.

EMOTIONAL CHANGES FROM ALCOHOL AND DRUGS

Within seconds of sipping an alcoholic drink, dopamine neurotransmitters in the brain convey pleasure. This change in brain chemistry lifts our mood, deadens stress and eases any uncomfortable feelings. Drinking more alcohol increases confidence and social ease. However, when intoxicated, we may say and do things we would swerve away from if sober. After just two drinks, dopamine's pleasure sensations can create intense cravings for more alcohol.

It can feel like alcohol makes us happier—and it does—for a while. But alcohol, by nature, is a depressant, and over-consumption often leads to feeling blue, sad or even maudlin.

Trauma, life events and all kinds of circumstances can result in the body's natural rhythms and chemistry becoming off balance, leading to prolonged anxiety and depression. As well as talking therapy, doctors may prescribe antidepressants. Most antidepressants stimulate the creation of serotonin and noradrenaline. These neurotransmitters are active in mood management and sleep—helping the body restore its natural balance.

As well as alcohol and caffeine, some over-the-counter medications and illegal drugs heighten, excite, dampen or calm our emotional state. Moderate consumption of alcohol and caffeine is easily tolerated by the body, yet they may be impacting you more than you realise.

SUMMARY OF EMOTIONAL MESSAGES

This book looks in detail at our emotional states in different scenarios, but here is quick summary of the messages that emotions convey to us.

Anger in all of its guises, tells us a boundary has been crossed. Its high vibrational energy, especially in full flow, provides the drive to restore trampled-over boundaries.

Fear arises to help us survive and stay safe. Fear is intricately woven into our intuition. When fear has no ebb and flow, it can be difficult to tell what is and isn't safe, which can lead to chronic anxiety.

Sadness arises from loss. Sadness deepens into grief after the death of a loved one. Compared to anger's fiery passion, sadness has low vibrational energy, providing time to slow down and reflect.

Shame and guilt are often used interchangeably to explain how we feel about times when we did not show up as our best self. Some argue that guilt is knowing the act was wrong, while shame comes up when we feel we have been caught out. Learning to work with shame's restorative energy lessens its impact on us and others we may have hurt.

Envy and jealousy are often synonymous too, yet these are quite different. Jealousy arises when we perceive—or know—that someone we love is showing attention and fondness for someone else. Envy arises when we perceive lack when comparing ourselves to others who appear to have abundance of what we desire.

Apathy, surprisingly, is suppressed anger. When it feels unsafe to express the higher intensity forms of anger, apathy arises to keep us safe, both from others and from ourselves.

Hurt, angry and not ready to forgive?

If you can find it in yourself to forgive,
then you are no longer chained
to the perpetrator.
♥ Archbishop, Desmond Tutu

Thomas Hardy aptly described my adopted home of Fortuneswell as:

Houses above houses, one man's doorstep rising behind his
neighbour's chimney, the gardens hung up by one edge to the sky.

Fortuneswell is a village on the Isle of Portland in Dorset. The houses are crammed together, with many streets so narrow and steep that driving up or down them for the first time is quite scary. Sitting halfway up a cliff, the village overlooks Chesil Beach. Most of the houses are built from Portland Stone, which was also used to build St Paul's Cathedral, Buckingham Palace and even parts of the United Nations Building in New York. There is, though, no grandeur on Portland. Over the centuries, millions of tons of Portland Stone have been carried off the island. Scars from the quarrying are still visible, yet most of the old hewn rocks are now softened by a green cloak of grass, moss and shrubs. In the spring, a profusion of wildflowers appear that makes the island beautiful, if not pretty. And Chesil Beach is stunning. Soon after moving to Weymouth, I fell in love with The Rock—the island's nickname. After decades of living in so many different places, I now can't imagine living anywhere else.

My home, The Jasmine House, is part of a terrace built in the 1850s. It is four storeys high and has large Georgian windows to the front. Because it is taller than it is wide, the house doesn't appear to be big, but it goes back a long way. When you go inside, it's a bit like entering Dr Who's TARDIS.

More important than its stature is what it feels like inside. The exterior walls, which at the front are fifteen inches thick, are built with Portland Stone. This makes inside peacefully quiet. The house was built on a three-inch scale, with walls, doors and windows positioned on an exact multiple of three. This symmetry creates a calming effect. So, when clients come to stay with me for a retreat, the house provides healing energy too.

The Sky Room is up on the fourth floor. It stretches from one side of the house to the other. To the front, a dormer window reveals a lovely view over the rooftops to the cliffs of Tophill. Yet this view hardly gets a look in as to the back, through a bank of Velux windows, there is an amazing view of Chesil Beach, the Fleet, Weymouth and rolling hills of Dorset. The Sky Room is where I work with my clients. It's also where I spend most of my time.

On one side of the room are two upright armchairs covered in fabric with a bright flower pattern. A small table sits between the chairs. My clients and I sit here when we work together. On the table, there is always a lit candle and a box of tissues ready, just in case they are needed.

STORIES THAT BREAK YOUR HEART

When a client first enters the Sky Room, their first word is always *Wow!* This is mostly because from street level there is no indication you can see the sea from the house, let alone in such a stunning fashion. Even in winter when it can be grey it's still inspiring. After enjoying the vista for a moment, we sit together, and I then sometimes catch a silent pause as they check whether it's safe to share their story. Some hold my gaze. Others look down at the carpet. I wait—there is no rush. Some have told their heart-breaking tale many times over and are reticent about once more diving into the depths. For others, it is their first time, and the moment is daunting. Everyone who comes on a retreat wishes to tell their story, to be understood and heard.

Often clients begin by telling me what's currently causing distress for them. It is only later we may discover old patterns that are influencing today's difficulties. Occasionally, clients immediately dive into the hurt because there is a huge desire to feel better; they want to be happy again and stop carrying their history of pain, but they don't know how to let go. Frequently, as they tell their story, their eyes glisten and silent tears roll down their cheeks as grief over what has been lost comes back up to the surface.

Over the years, I have listened to many stories that began in childhood when their dad, mum, uncle, brother or grandfather physically or sexually abused them. Sometimes it's not a family member but a family friend or a leader of children's activities. And sometimes my client is the parent of the abused child. In these cases, they are wracked with guilt, blaming themselves for not spotting what was happening to their son or daughter.

In physical and sexual abuse, men are more likely, but not always, the perpetrator. Both men and women inflict mental and emotional abuse. If a child doesn't receive enough care, guidance or love due to one or both parents being in pain or an addict, as an adult, they often feel unworthy and not good enough.

Although emotional trauma in childhood is common, many women have told me how their husbands, when drunk, have raped them. Far more than you might imagine have told me how their partner attempted to strangle them, put a knife to their throat or kicked them in the stomach while pregnant.

One of my clients told me he had begun hiding under his desk after his colleagues left for the day. He said he was so stressed that this was the only place that felt safe. In our work together, we uncovered that as a very young child he used to hide under the kitchen table, which was draped with a long table cloth. He had been petrified of his mother, who regularly hit him for little or no reason.

How can any human being inflict this much pain on another adult—or worse still on a child? Why in our supposedly civilised society is this *still* happening? Poverty, alcoholism or misuse of drugs account for some atrocious behaviours, yet mostly it's not this. Children and adults from all walks of life are maltreated. Wealth and a good education sadly don't necessarily prevent this from happening either.

Being harmed or abused, or witnessing or being involved in tragic or horrific events, changes who you are. These events create an emotional wound which just like a physical wound needs to heal. How long it takes to heal depends on what happened, whether you received support, and your personality. Trust your own knowing about this. If what happened to you caused pain and it still lingers, it matters. And it needs to heal.

YOU ARE NOT THE ONLY ONE

The NSPCC—a leading UK charity dedicated to preventing cruelty to children—estimates that more than one in ten adults have survived some form of childhood abuse. Consider that for a moment. One in ten people at your workplace. One in ten amongst your friends. One in ten of everyone you know.

We often don't know who these people are because the stigma of sharing such stories is too great. Most survivors with a painful past become masters of disguise. Some become the life and soul of the party. Others take on the role of a clown. More commonly, they show up as private or shy people.

Even those who are gregarious may keep people at arm's length. The fear of being hurt again keeps the barriers up.

Unhealed pain can remain in the psyche for months, years or even decades. There is truth in the old saying that time is a healer, but when pain pierces a heart, it will not entirely go away until inner peace is found.

I've not analysed how many of my clients have suffered from abuse, neglect, betrayal, rape, fear-induced control or violence. My guess is that it's one in three. What I know is that it happens far too often.

My clients are actively wanting to heal and feel better—happier. Many of them have survived and done so well despite everything that has happened to them. Many of them choose to embark on a healing journey that may take years or a lifetime to complete. To work with them—to walk with them along this challenging stretch of their life—is humbling. At the same time, I desperately want these atrocities to stop so in generations to come, abuse and harm will be rare occurrences. And for that to happen, the perpetrators need help too.

INSIGHTS FROM THOSE IN PRISON

It's true that too many perpetrators get away with what they have done. It has to change—yet many who inflict pain are suffering too. This doesn't make what they did right. Nor is their pain an excuse. Hurting someone else is never justifiable. However, statistics about prisoners' early life is revealing. A Ministry of Justice study, *Prisoners' childhood and family backgrounds 2012* (as of 2023, this is still the most up-to-date report), questioned 3,849 prisoners. The results showed 29% had suffered childhood abuse, 24% had been in care at some point, 41% had witnessed severe abuse or alcoholism, and 37% had one parent who had been convicted of a criminal offence. Several of these factors for any one prisoner overlapped. The lack of care given to our most vulnerable children is partly what pushes them over the edge into criminality and, for some, why they begin to inflict pain on others.

THE CYCLE OF HARM

Long before I forgave my granddad, given a chance, I would have put him in prison and thrown away the key. But now, understanding more about how abuse and harm occur, the picture is not so black and white.

Although there is some blurring of the lines, there are generally three outcomes after surviving an abusive event. The first is that the one who was hurt becomes a person who hurts others. *How can that be true?* Logic would assume that starting to hurt others is the last thing someone would do after being hurt themselves. Yet, virtually all abusers were once themselves abused. Most abusers are men. Other common predictors of those who harm others later in life include growing up in an environment where violence towards women was considered acceptable. Or in childhood they witnessed violence, alcoholism, drug use, and or received a poor education. In many cases, perpetrators strive to control another person through pain, humiliation or subjugation to make themselves feel better. Being once more in control feels good to them—at least temporarily. You can find more information on this topic by searching for the *Domestic Abuse Plan* on www.gov.uk.

Some bullies realise the extent of the hurt they have inflicted. Typically— and most times genuinely—they are filled with remorse and beg for forgiveness. They say they will never do it again, but often another trigger leads to a repeat performance. Without professional intervention, this cycle will, sadly, continue.

In other instances, abusers twist their stories, believing that participation in these acts is mutually desired. My granddad frequently told me he loved me and asked me if I loved him too. In his perverted way, I think this is how he justified what he did to me.

The second way is to take on the role of a victim. During the traumatic event, it was most likely impossible to stop what was happening. Yet afterwards, the feeling of helplessness is overwhelming. This is frequently met with self-recrimination; thoughts such as *Why could I not stop it? Why didn't I yell or kick to escape?* Shame is often the biggest block that keeps victimhood in the psyche.

Those who were bullied, abused or controlled may unconsciously adopt victimhood as a means of staying safe. By acting small, it might act as a shield against getting hurt. And, surprisingly, we may uncover victimhood in ourselves. As a swan, what is going on under the surface is so well hidden that most people don't see our pain. To mask our pain, we may be the one who always goes above and beyond to help our family, work colleagues and friends. We may prioritise their needs while ours remain at the bottom of the pile. Yet these kind acts and hard work may not be unconditional giving. Rather, it may be a way of receiving praise, to once more feel appreciated and also safe in belonging. However, if recognition for our kind acts is not forthcoming, then we may begin to blame others for not doing their fair share of the work—even when we gladly offered or even volunteered to do the task.

A dance between people on different paths after trauma may result in unhealthy adult relationships. For example, in co-dependent relationships where one is narcissistic and the other a rescuer. The person who controls may appear stronger—and sometimes they are—yet underneath the mask, most are as scared as the person they are hurting or controlling.

The third and best way forward after surviving abuse or harm is to embark on a journey to heal this pain. Speaking about what happened, examining it, coming to understand it from all perspectives eventually brings a moment when it is possible to let go. It can sometimes be done under your own steam, but for those who have suffered, it often requires working with a professional. No matter which path you take to heal, it is not about forgetting what happened—rather, it is about moving on without the old burdens.

FORGIVENESS SETS YOU FREE

It's hard to forgive someone who has done horrible things to you. It may feel repugnant even to consider it. Why should *you* forgive *them*—when you did nothing wrong? It feels like *they* should be asking for forgiveness. Yet, finding a way to forgive them allows you to accept what happened without the earlier fears, shame or anger that was felt.

The biggest misconception around forgiveness is the belief it pardons the person who caused harm. While it may include this, forgiveness is not for them—it's for you. It's a way to release them from *your* thoughts so that both consciously and subconsciously there is a sense of closure and completion. Forgiveness categorically does not condone what was done. Where appropriate, the person should pay for their crimes through the legal system.

Forgiveness means reaching the point where you no longer hold animosity, resentment, indignation, anger or hatred for the indiscretion, harm or violation that you experienced at the hands of another. It takes strength and courage to forgive and let go of what happened. It's most definitely not a sign of weakness.

I've read accounts of people instantly forgiving a stranger who caused harm to them or their family. I admire these people because it is hard to do. I sense that these people understand the freeing nature of forgiveness.

For most people, the journey to forgiveness takes time, especially where there are conflicting emotions due to knowing the person, as well as a lack of justice. Alongside everything else, there is usually the unanswered question of, *Why did this happen to me?* Rarely is there a logical answer, but it doesn't stop the question from coming back up.

EVA MOZES KOR'S STORY

On YouTube, you can find many videos of Eva Mozes Kor's story of forgiveness. It may inspire you to see that even the worst of the worst can be forgiven.

In 1944, Eva's family were taken to Auschwitz with many other Jewish families. They travelled there in a cattle truck on a train. When they arrived, Nazi soldiers herded them onto a crowded platform. Eva became separated from her mother, father and brothers, and she never saw them again. Eva and her twin sister Miriam were chosen to take part in Dr Mengele's cruel medical experiments on twins—over 3,000 of them. On many occasions, either Eva or Miriam were injected with, or were forced to take mediations, using the other as control study. Many times, they were perilously ill, yet they both survived and were released from the camp in 1945.

In 1995, to mark fifty years since the death camp's liberation, Eva talked about how she first found a way to forgive a Nazi doctor. Her friend, who had been helping her to do this, then challenged her to forgive Dr Mengele too. She asked Eva to imagine Mengele in the room with her when she forgave him, and importantly, to notice how she felt when she did so. Eva recalled the moment.

'I picked up my dictionary and first wrote down 20 nasty words, which I read clear and loud to that make-believe Mengele in the room. At the end, I said, in spite [of] all that, I forgive you. It made me feel very good. That I, the little guinea-pig of 50 years ago, even had the power over the Angel of Death at Auschwitz.'

She continued to say that she realised no one could ever take this power away from her and that at last she no longer felt like his victim.

BREAKING THE CHAIN

The quotation at the start of this chapter by Archbishop Desmond Tutu is part of a longer passage, which you can find via www.theforgivenessproject.com. He writes:

When I talk of forgiveness, I mean the belief that you can come out the other side a better person. A better person than the one being consumed by anger and hatred. Remaining in that state locks you in a state of victimhood, making you almost dependent on the perpetrator. If you can find it in yourself to forgive, then you are no longer chained to the perpetrator. You can move on, and you can even help the perpetrator to become a better person too.

When Desmond Tutu says, *no longer chained to the perpetrator*, he means everything—not just the event but also how it has impacted your life. By forgiving someone who has caused you pain, you are set free—the old ties, which may include anger, shame, sadness and fear, drop away.

WHY DID THEY DO WHAT THEY DID?

You may remember that as part of my healing, Joel asked me questions about Granddad to help me see him beyond the monster I had painted him to be. Through this, I realised my love of gardening and flowers began with Granddad. The produce from his vegetable plot and his greenhouses were my grandparents' only source of income. Yet, he gave valuable space in the greenhouse to grow geraniums and carnations simply because he loved their beauty.

Who was my granddad, really? I still don't know. But my dad was a kind, hard-working, generous man who believed in truth and fairness. If my granddad was evil incarnate, how did my dad turn out so well? When I considered this conundrum, the massive contradiction wasn't easy to accept. In forgiving Granddad, I had to see his humanity. I had to acknowledge that he was not full of darkness—that even within him, a light shone.

When the hurt has been inflicted by a family member, friend, or friend of the family, the healing has to include unravelling the confusing mixture of love and hate. In cases of sexual abuse, grooming includes giving attention, gifts and tenderness—some of which is genuine. It's not black and white in these instances—it's more like a murky grey.

In relatively rarer cases, when a stranger has attacked or raped someone, the healing includes exploring *Why me?* Often this is impossible to answer because for the attacker it was an opportunistic moment.

The person who did what was done is often painted as the monster—and for what they have done, they are. Yet, it is rare to consider who they are beyond the abusive acts. What led them to do what they did? What triggered their behaviour? Why did they do it? Taking some time to explore these questions can help you begin seeing them as people, not just the act or acts they performed.

HOW DO YOU FORGIVE SOMEONE?

Forgiveness happens when you can literally or mentally look the person in the eye and say, *I forgive you.* To do this means finding compassion in your heart for the person who hurt you and seeing their humanity. No one is perfect. We may not have wounded another in such a terrible way, but we have all hurt someone during our life.

Consider and ask whether they acted deliberately or maliciously. Did their childhood make them capable of doing this to you?

Forgiveness takes time, and it is a layered process. For example, when a survivor forgives a perpetrator, it's often followed by a surge of relief. This may, though, be temporary as the floodgates open with hurt for the length of time spent suffering. Or having forgiven the one who hurt you, there may be new hurt at feeling unprotected by someone else who perhaps could have stopped it happening. Honour each layer of forgiveness. In time, it becomes more comfortable, and there will be a growing awareness of how to find peace with it all.

One of the joys of forgiveness is that you step back into your own power. The perpetrator no longer has any control over you or any rights in your life.

FORGIVING YOURSELF

My story included the need to forgive myself for all the guilt I had carried around with me for decades. It did not matter that I wasn't the guilty one—I felt it, and I had carried it with me.

In your story, despite it not being your fault, do you need to forgive yourself too? Not for what was or was not done, but perhaps for how you weren't able to stop it or weren't able to tell anyone. Remember you survived, and you are here today. Be gentle with your precious soul. Don't be harsh with yourself if there is still a lot of healing to be done. Your forgiveness journey is what it is. Maybe today is the day you begin to forgive what happened. Maybe you will be ready by tomorrow.

BEGIN YOUR JOURNEY OF FORGIVENESS

Have you ever had the chance to say how you really feel about what happened to you? It can be cathartic to write your story. Try this exercise of writing a letter.

WRITE A LETTER

This letter will not be posted. It is, though, addressed to and written as if it was going to be read by the person who hurt you. I recommend writing your letter by hand, as it can help you channel your energies more directly. In your letter, tell the person how it was through your eyes. Let them know the impact of their actions on your life. Write how you feel without editing or being polite. Let it all flow out and through you. When you have finished, keep the letter for a few days. Add to it if something else comes to mind. Read it over and over until you are satisfied that everything has been said. Then, pick a time to honour this process, and take your letter into a garden, park or any place where it is safe to burn it. As you watch the edges of the paper turn brown and the words curl up into the smoke, feel the power that person has had on you, being released.

The healing power of anger

*Anger is like flowing water
—there's nothing wrong with it
as long as you let it flow.*
♥ C. JoyBell C.

When anger ignites within, it can lead us to do or say the meanest things. In a heated moment, we don't much care about the pain we're inflicting or the repercussions. It's only later that shame arises to let us know we could have handled it better. Even in its quieter tone, anger can still feel uncomfortable as we don't know how to process this powerful emotion.

Anger is, perhaps, the most misunderstood emotion. Many people believe anger is bad and frown on those who publicly lose their cool. Yet everyone, even the calmest of people, has experienced anger. Like all emotions, anger conveys a message about what is going on in our lives. Anger tells us a boundary has been pushed, stepped over or crushed. The greater the boundary infringement, the more intense our emotional response will be. Anger's purpose is to restore and make our boundaries strong. Once a boundary is back in place, anger naturally dissipates.

Anger goes awry when it's suppressed, ignored or dismissed. Pushing anger back inside is only ever a temporary solution. Anger's fire can't be put out without an outlet. With anger simmering inside, it may seep out in sarcastic, snide or unkind remarks. Held-on-to anger will, sometimes, erupt like a volcano, and the words spewed-out out will be destructive as any lava flow. Sadly, anger like this will not necessarily land on the person you are angry with. Sometimes, this wrath lands on a loved one.

One of my early retreat clients, Joe, had been struggling with his temper—and his anger often landed on his girlfriend, when she wasn't the originator of his fury.

JOE'S STORY

Joe arrived at The Jasmine House on a cold, crisp morning in January. On the doorstep, he smiled and shook my hand. As I welcomed him in, I guessed Joe was in his early thirties. His accent sounded Australian, although I knew he was living in and had travelled from London. Tall, with a mop of dark curly hair, Joe wore jeans, an Arran jumper and no jacket, despite the cold air.

Today, when people book a retreat, we will meet first on Zoom, so I have a better idea of what has happened or is happening in their lives. But pre-pandemic, and long before I had heard of Zoom, at my request, people would send me an email. Some people wrote reams. Some just made a list of short bullet-points, while yet others ticked the option to tell me more when they arrived. Joe and I had a conversation covering the logistics, but before he arrived, I had no sense of what had spurred him to book a retreat with me.

On the day of Joe's arrival, I led the way to the Sky Room. As we climbed the stairs, I idly wondered where this afternoon session with Joe would go. Three flights up, the stairs come directly into the Sky Room. Like all of my clients, Joe stopped in his tracks with a *Wow!* As he admired the panorama of Chesil Beach.

I motioned for Joe to sit in an armchair facing the windows so he could continue to see the view. I opened my notebook.

'Let's begin. What are you hoping to get from your retreat, Joe?'

He pulled a folded piece of paper from his jeans pocket and opened it. I could see he had prepared a bullet-point list, which he read to me;

* Clarity about the direction of my career.
* Learn how to manage my workload better.
* Decide whether or not to move back to Melbourne.
* Stop feeling like I'm not good enough at my job.

He paused and looked directly at me before continuing:

* Stop losing my temper with Julie.

I scribbled his list into my notebook.

'That will keep us busy,' I teased before gently adding, 'Out of curiosity, Joe, do you do that a lot—lose your temper, that is?'

Joe dropped his eyes from my gaze. 'Yes.'

'More with Julie—or more at work?'

Joe's eyes darted around the room. 'Work stresses me out, but I'm cool with it. I don't lose it.'

I nodded and with curiosity rising, I continued my queries.

'What stresses you at work, Joe?' Then taking an intuitive leap, I added, 'I'm wondering, is there some hidden anger beneath the stress at work?'

Joe crossed his arms, and I waited. It can be challenging to see a different picture from the one in your head. Beginning to explore a new reality, especially one you don't like, takes time to process. I held a warm silence for Joe while he considered my question.

Joe uncrossed his arms, 'Perhaps,' he said quietly.

He caught my eye and added, 'I was taught not to express anger—Dad said it was a weakness to get angry with a woman—so when I lose my temper with Julie, it upsets me. But at work...' His voice trailed off.

We were diving into the deep end, and I sensed he was slightly unnerved by the speed we had begun talking about his feelings.

For a moment, Joe was lost in the view through the window. Then he came back and continued, '... there are lots of things that are stressful at work. But we all have to deal with these things. Best to just get on with it.'

'No, Joe—not if it's causing this level of stress. When anger arises, it is trying to tell you things are not OK. If we push anger back inside of us, its energy builds up until, one day, it explodes. Then we might take it out on those we love—even though it's not about them. Afterwards, we feel awful and vow we'll never do it again. But often we do.'

As I spoke, I noticed Joe's head slightly nodding along with my words. I saw how anger was causing such a lot of internal conflict.

Over the next few days, I worked with Joe on his anger using EFT—Emotional Freedom Technique. EFT is a tapping therapy that helps people let go of long-held emotions. The tapping stimulates the body's energy system, while the spoken words enable rapid changes about what is felt regarding a particular event, situation or circumstance. EFT doesn't wipe away memories of past events; rather it changes how we feel about what happened to us.

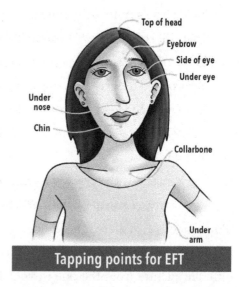

Tapping points for EFT

For Joe, we began with what seemed pretty innocuous—his constantly-full in-tray at work. As we tapped, this brought up how much he hated his inconsiderate and unappreciative boss for forever increasing his workload. So, then we tapped on Joe's hatred of his boss. Following that, Joe told me he was pissed off with the Friday afternoon sales meetings. He mumbled,

I'm not on the sales team—why do I have to be there? Joe was also cross with a colleague who, he said, was on a mission to discredit his work while taking the glory for himself.

With each revelation, the intensity of his emotions surprised Joe. He had not realised just how much he had been storing inside. Like popping the cork of a champagne bottle, Joe's anger was bubbling up. As we examined each layer, we explored the whys and tapped to release the anger. Increasingly, Joe realised the degree of disrespect his boss demonstrated towards him and many of his colleagues. Finally, in our last session, I noticed Joe looked calmer and more at peace.

'You've worked through a lot, Joe—well done!'

I smiled and added, 'But we haven't much spoken about Julie. Now you're clearer about work, I'm wondering if you feel differently about her?'

Joe smiled back.

'I think I was taking my work frustrations out on Julie without realising it. I think it's more whether I return home to Melbourne—which Mum keeps nagging me about—or whether I stay in London. I don't know how Julie fits into all of this if I go home.'

Joe didn't make any firm decisions before leaving. He knew he needed to consider what to do about work as the current situation was untenable. Without carrying all of the anger, Joe could now have conversations with both his mum and Julie about the future.

MORE ABOUT ANGER

Anger is rarely about one thing. Even when there is one incident, it's often connected to earlier events. Then, the old anger and the new combine, intensifying the feelings. Or, if it's too much to bear, we may disassociate. Or we may channel our anger in one direction, deflecting it from what's happening, as Joe had done.

Unless we have been taught—which is rare—most of us don't know how to process anger in a healthy way. So, instead, we process anger on instinct and what we learned in our formative years. Children who were regularly yelled at in anger often mimic their parent's behaviour when they become adults, despite knowing it's neither rational nor helpful. Likewise, those whose parents never expressed anger tend not to address their anger later in life. The latter might appear to be a better approach—and it could be—yet never expressing anger can be equally problematic. Anger acts as a sentinel to our boundaries. Without this protective energy, it may be difficult to define or defend boundaries that keep us safe.

Being happy and at peace doesn't exclude feeling angry. Instead, anger and other challenging emotions play an important role in in our life. These emotions convey powerful messages, and they can change our life in a good way. Cultivating a healthy way of dealing with anger gives it a voice without harming ourselves or anyone else.

How safe and happy you feel often indicates how easily or not anger is triggered. Another factor is your level of self-esteem at the moment. For example, imagine walking on a crowded pavement. Someone barges into you, their shoulder bashing yours as they walk by, and they don't say sorry. If you feel happy and safe, this event may cause nothing more than an utterance, and then it's forgotten. Or it may awaken compassionate curiosity as to why they were so distracted to ignore social norms. However, if this same incident occurs when you're stressed, anxious or vulnerable, it may trigger anger. The barging feels threatening—an invasion of personal space—which needs defending. And so your reaction might be to shout, or shake a fist at the passing stranger's back.

APATHY: ANGER'S MASK OF INDIFFERENCE

When a client says they never get angry, even when their story is full of boundaries smashed to smithereens, I'm curious as to why. Is their righteous anger lurking beneath the surface? Is it being masked with apathy or boredom? It's not that I want people to be angry—I don't! But a complete lack of anger may lead to being apathetic or lethargic, in which case something is probably lurking in the depths.

Apathy arises to hide anger when a situation is too scary to tackle. Or it feels impossible to speak out. In this way, apathy plays a protective role. Yet, in these instances, anger hasn't gone away—it's merely hiding, leaving a lack-lustre energy in its place.

When apathy becomes stuck inside, it shows up as boredom, along with a continual search for something new. This desire may be searching for a new job, wanting a better relationship, wanting to move, or even a new hairstyle. Yet, with apathy lingering, the delight of the new quickly wears off, instigating the search for another distraction. Never feeling satisfied may be due to apathy. Becoming aware of these feelings often signifies it's time to find a safe way to allow anger to have its voice.

EXERCISES TO DEAL WITH ANGER

Lashing out in anger is never helpful. And it is horrible if you're on the receiving end of it. So, how can anger be processed healthily? How is it possible to stay dignified and yet say, *No, this is not OK with me.*

The first step in clearing anger is to become crystal clear about the intensity of your anger. Read down the list on the next page. Which form of anger resonates the most? Does your anger primarily reside at the top or the bottom of the list? If none of these words feels appropriate to you, take a moment to check again. No one wants to admit to being angry. Yet, life will continually throw niggling events, obstacles and different points of view across your path.

Start this first exercise by considering a recent situation that ruffled your feathers. Now, write a sentence that describes precisely how you feel. Try a sentence similar to those on the next page.

ANGER
Irritated
Annoyed
Cross
Frustrated
Angry
Exasperated
Furious
Incensed
Bitter
Livid
Seething
Vindictive
Raging
Apoplectic
Red Mist

* Susan didn't deserve the promotion! I am seething—she just waltzed in and took this job from me.
* Jim is always late. I am frustrated that I keep wasting my precious time waiting for him to arrive.
* I feel exasperated with Dalia. Why does she keep taking advantage of me? She simply doesn't appreciate how much I do for her.

What is your anger sentence? How does it feel to see it in black and white? Now check-in with yourself. Is there another emotion wrapped around anger? Fear and sadness often dance with anger, especially if there are potentially unpleasant consequences.

Pinning down your anger and giving it a specific name stops it from being so nebulous, making it easier to process.

When angry—first learn to walk away: This is, of course, much easier to say than do. Anger triggers our survival instincts. When this happens, we have less access to rational thought. But by setting an intention before it happens, we are far more likely to succeed in those nanoseconds before our survival instincts take over.

Walking away allows everyone to have a time-out. Tackling the situation can happen the next day, week or even a few weeks later. A time-out allows everyone to be more objective. When you revisit the subject, they may be remorseful, or they may be able to express their views more rationally. However, this will not always be the case. You can't control what they do or say, but you can choose to be responsible for your words.

Dealing with red mist: With great gentleness and honesty, reflect on any recent angry outbursts. Did your anger spiral out of control into an irrational and uncontrollable rage? Did red mist descend, and afterwards, was it difficult to recall what was said?

Intense feelings of insecurity are often the culprit beneath the red mist. Every boundary infringement feels like a threat to safety. Words or fists are used to stay safe and keep demons at arm's length. Hurled words upset the person in the firing zone and your precious soul too. In such instances, after anger has lost its energy, allow shame's energy to arise, which helps you to put things right.

Channelling your anger: This means finding a safe space to allow anger to flow through you and reveal what is really going on. Channelling means processing anger instead of taking it out on someone else.

To begin this process, you must first match anger's fiery energy by doing something to get your heart pumping faster. Do anything that works for you—a brisk walk, a jog, a fast cycle ride or a cardio workout at the gym. Whichever method you use, when your heart is beating faster than usual, with each stride, push or pull, with emphasis and an angry tone to your voice, say, *I am angry*. Keep repeating this until you feel a surge of anger enter your mind and body—it rarely takes long. Now it's time to ask yourself these questions:

* Who am I angry with?
* What needs to be restored?

In response to, *Who am I angry with?* notice how your heart beats faster as a name instantly come to mind. To the question, *What needs to be restored?* the answer is nearly always *Me—I need to be restored*.

At this point, take a few deep breaths, then ask yourself the final question,

What needs to change? Make a note of your responses, either immediately or when you arrive home. As you review your answers, do you still feel angry? Or as angry as you were before? Surprisingly, for most people, anger will have greatly dissipated after this simple exercise. Knowing the root cause of anger, being crystal clear about it, is a huge step forward as to how to resolve the situation. So, anger's role is at least partly fulfilled.

In terms of what needs to be changed—what can you do? Do you need to talk to the person involved? Or, now it has been considered—maybe you no longer need or want to do anything? Ensure, though, it's not fear that is pushing the anger back inside. If talking directly to the person isn't possible, could a supervisor, boss, leader or family member facilitate the conversation? As you process what you wish to do, make sure there is no hidden agenda, vindictiveness or a desire for revenge. Succumbing to a desire to get your own back will, in some way, backfire, making things worse.

Finally, consider what is needed to make this right for you. Do you need an apology? Will you be happy if the person who has irked/infuriated you meets you halfway? If a desire for vengeance pops back up, wait another day for it to pass, and then do the channelling process again. The second time around may uncover more to the story, and you can use these insights to help you put things right.

If anger doesn't dissipate but intensifies, or you are frequently losing yourself in a red mist, please don't feel dismayed. Instead, recognise there is more work to be done. We all have areas of life that require more self-development. And, if this is you, perhaps consider finding a therapist to help you.

Restore your boundaries

*Daring to set boundaries is about
having the courage to love ourselves,
even when we risk disappointing others.*
♥ Brené Brown

Have you ever said yes or silently agreed to something when you wanted to say no? Was it just too difficult to say what you felt at that moment? We say yes when we want to say no for many reasons. Often, it is because we don't want to let people down. Sometimes, we are scared of saying what we truly feel in case doing so makes everything go pear-shaped. Or we want to be helpful and responsible—even if we already have too much on our plate.

A good amount of give-and-take is needed for harmonious living. However, there are times when it is important to stand up for your beliefs and values. The tricky part is finding the right balance. Being dogmatic and standing up for every infringement of your values will create a battleground. Being too lax will puncture self-esteem, and others may take advantage of your kind nature. Finding this balance begins with a deeper understanding of boundaries.

WHAT ARE BOUNDARIES?

Boundaries are your lines in the sand that you believe should not be crossed by others. With strong, healthy boundaries in place, you have a safe space to be your authentic self. Boundaries can be identified by words, actions or behaviour directed towards you that instinctively make you want to say, *No—that's not OK with me.*

Some boundary lines are obvious. Everyone is going to say no to hurtful, harmful and abusive behaviour. But what about teasing? Does it feel OK to be teased? Or when you meet a friend who always turns up late—is that a boundary issue for you? What about when your work colleague leaves on time and you stay behind to complete a joint project?

Our boundaries are as unique as our fingerprints. We rarely tell friends and family where our boundaries lie—yet we expect them to know them nonetheless. This is why we feel betrayed when someone we love crosses a line. In these moments, we are perplexed by their words or actions. And we may become like a petulant child who cries, *How could they say and do that!*

What is OK for some people is most definitely not OK for others. Let's look again at teasing. Some people relish teasing banter, seeing it as a form of affection. Others consider it disrespectful. Neither is right or wrong—our views are simply different. We share common values, yet we also have a myriad of our own. The same goes for our beliefs. Because of this, people may unknowingly trample over our boundaries, and we may do the same to them.

When we tell people what behaviour is OK—and what is not—most people will respect our boundaries even if they are different from theirs. But some won't—as happened to my client Simon—who was dealing with a straightforward yet hurtful boundary crossing.

SIMON'S STORY

Simon was clever. He had become a chartered accountant at twenty-four when most of his peers would not qualify for another year or more. Simon had been promoted to lead a small team at a local accountancy company, but he was struggling in this new role, and his boss asked me to be his Life Coach.

I met Simon at the accountancy firm's office in a nondescript business centre. He led me into the meeting room and then waited for me to sit at the table before taking a seat himself. His gangly body didn't entirely fill out his suit, but his delightful old-fashioned manners made him seem older than his years.

To begin our coaching session, I asked Simon what he liked about his new role and what he didn't. He told me he enjoyed visiting businesses to do an audit, as he was learning a lot. But he also felt undermined by some of his team, especially those older than him.

Catching Simon's gaze, I asked, 'If I waved my magic wand to make working with your team better, what would you wish for?'

In an instant, he replied, 'I'd like for everyone to call me Simon.'

Slightly puzzled, I asked him to tell me more.

'Everyone calls me Miller,' he explained, 'while everyone else is called by their first name. I hate it. I feel excluded.'

'That seems unfair. Do you know why they do this?'

Simon explained that his boss was also called Simon. Someone in the team, he couldn't remember who, began calling him Miller, and it had stuck.

'They probably have no idea how it's making you feel,' I ventured. 'What would it be like if your colleagues called you Simon?'

His smile told me all I needed to know. So, I suggested that he could call a team meeting, which he agreed to do. I taught Simon how to use Truth Talking—the technique is covered in the next chapter—but in essence, this helps you say what you are experiencing without casting blame. After explaining the method, we role-played the slightly unnatural words until Simon felt comfortable. By the end of our session, along with several other pointers, Simon had three sentences to deliver during his team meeting.

When we met the following week, Simon grinned as he shook my hand. He told me that the meeting had gone well, and most of the team were now calling him Simon. He said one of the bookkeepers had called him Miller again, but he reminded her, and she apologised, saying she had forgotten.

I could sense there was more.

'I noticed you said *most* of the team—is someone not playing ball?'

Simon sighed.

'It's Dave. He hates that I'm now a team leader. Dave and I trained together, but he failed his last exam.'

'Have you reminded him to call you Simon?'

'Yes, but now he seems to relish calling me Miller.'

I explained that while it's rare, some people choose to disrespect boundaries after they have been defined. I asked Simon if he was ready to defend his boundary—not just define it. He admitted to being a bit scared, but he agreed to give it go.

Later that week, finding the right moment, he approached Dave and used the words we had again formulated and practised. These were his three sentences.

'Dave, I have spoken to you about calling me, Miller. I find it disrespectful that you are continuing to do this. I need you to stop.'

And, as we had practised, Simon didn't give Dave a chance to reply. Instead, he simply walked away. Over the next few months, there were a few more run-ins with Dave, but for this boundary, Dave toed the line.

HOW DO YOU KNOW WHEN A BOUNDARY HAS BEEN CROSSED?

A boundary has been crossed when you experience an adverse reaction to words or actions spoken or done to you. The more you care about what was said or done, the more intense your emotional response will be. Anger will be present in one of its guises, as its role is to restore boundaries.

Entwined with anger, there will be other feelings such as vulnerability, embarrassment, anxiety, sadness or guilt.

Notice that you may experience similar emotions when reading, hearing or seeing people say or do things you feel are wrong. But, unless these are spoken or directed to you, they have not crossed *your* boundaries.

Simon's boundary was relatively easy to see, define and put right. It can, though, be far more complicated, as it was for another client, a young woman called Angie.

ANGIE'S STORY

The moment we sat down in the therapy chairs in the Sky Room, Angie blurted out, 'My life is such a mess.' And she began to cry.

Angie looked so very young. She was petite and wore skinny jeans with an oversized cream jumper, emphasising her vulnerability. She dabbed her eyes with a tissue pulled from the box I had offered her. As her tears kept rolling down her cheeks, her long, brown hair fell forward, hiding her face from me.

My heart went out to her. Angie had opted to wait until she was here before telling me why she had chosen to come on retreat. So, at this moment, I had no idea what had happened or what was going on for her, but it felt like she needed some reassurance.

'Life is sometimes messy, Angie. What has happened?'

Angie pushed back her hair and looked at me. Her brown eyes were full of sadness and, I sensed, desperation.

For the next hour, between sobs, big sighs, and sometimes noisily blowing her nose, I listened to her story. It took a while to sort it out as Angie jumped from one part of the story to another. I asked questions to gain clarity too. As with any account, tangents and extra detail sometimes clouded what was going on. So, the following is how I pieced together Angie's story.

It began when Angie's school choir had been invited to Washington, USA, to participate in a Choir Festival. Angie told me she had been excited and loved every moment of this experience—from helping to choose the songs and working on how they could be re-imagined to endless practising and getting comfortable with the simple choreography. The week before the trip, they did one last rehearsal, and the choirmaster smiled, finally satisfied with their performance. Angie told me it was more than just the festival—it was also her first time on a plane.

The festival included eight choirs—five schools from Washington and three from London. The day after Angie and her friends arrived, all the choirs, choir directors, and supervising teachers gathered in a huge auditorium. Angie described the room. There were chairs with padded cushions arranged into groups for each choir. A large stage had a grand piano to one side, while in the centre, there were microphones on stands and, above, rows of spotlights. It was very different from Angie's modest, multifunctional school hall.

The hosting school choir opened the competition with a clever a-cappella of Katy Perry's *Teenage Dream*. Angie told me she had goosebumps when she heard the lead singer's soulful voice. He commanded the song, and she was instantly drawn to his good looks and unusual strawberry-blond hair.

Naturally shy, Angie had felt more confident in this new place where no one knew who she was. During the lunch break, everyone went to the school cafeteria. The contrast with Angie's school was again stark as it felt more like a restaurant. Angie spotted the lead singer of the hosting choir, and impulsively, she walked over to him. With newfound courage, Angie smiled and told him she was a fan of Katy Perry and that she loved how they had reworked the song. He smiled broadly, introducing himself as Jackson—but told her, *everyone calls me Jack*. He invited her to pull up a chair and join him and his friends.

Over the next few days, Angie cleverly orchestrated bumping into Jack whenever there was a break. She wasn't sure whether Jack knew what she was doing, but he welcomed her into his posse. Jack was a joker, making everyone laugh with his awful but instantly recognisable impersonations of the choir directors. He told her he loved her accent. Angie discovered he was impulsive and charming to both his friends and teachers. Angie noticed that one of the girls in his choir, Mary-Ann, seemed to hang on to his every word. In Jack's absence, Mary-Ann had several times told Angie she didn't belong and told her, *Go back to your choir*. Yet it seemed that Jack increasingly sought out Angie's company too.

On the last day, there was a sightseeing trip. The hosting school choir acted as tour guides. Jack made sure he was with Angie's group. The last stop was at the Lincoln Memorial, and Jack had reached out and squeezed Angie's hand.

That evening, a farewell party was held in the auditorium. The chairs now lined the walls around the wooden floor. A young DJ tried his best to get everyone dancing but with little success. Angie hadn't minded because she was sitting beside Jack, listening to the banter between him and his friends.

Jack had brazenly brought beer for the evening, smuggled into the auditorium in metal water bottles hidden in his rucksack. He had poured beer into everyone's white plastic cups. Unaccustomed to alcohol, Angie, Jack and his friends were soon tipsy. Jack winked at Angie, held out his hand to her, and then whisked her onto the dance floor. Jack parodied rock and roll, making Angie feel both special and cool.

Later, Jack retook Angie's hand and led her through the now melee of gyrating, dancing bodies. At the side of the stage, Jack opened a small door. A few steps took them into a well-lit corridor. There was access beneath the stage on one side, on the other side, two more doors. Jack opened one of these, which was a small storage room. In the dim light filtering through a slither of a window near the ceiling, Angie saw stacks of chairs and stage props. Jack turned to Angie and kissed her—gently at first, then more passionately. Angie responded, and their entwined bodies half walked, half fell onto a plastic-covered sofa. The plastic cover squeaked loudly in protest, and for a moment, they lay still, both afraid the noise would alert someone. Then laughter engulfed them—no one could hear anything over the loud music. More kisses and fumbling followed, and then, half-undressed, they had sex.

Angie didn't tell Jack it was her first time. In the moment, she felt alive, exhilarated and sexy. And yet, afterwards, Angie felt a stab of regret. Making love in a storage room was not how she had envisaged losing her virginity. But Jack had grinned at her, kissed her forehead and helped her straighten her dress. Despite her misgivings, it had been special because it was with Jack. They smiled inanely at one another before sneaking back into the auditorium.

Mary-Ann seemed to have been the only one who had realised they were missing. As they headed back to the group, she brushed passed Angie and whispered *slut*. Soon the DJ announced it was the last dance. Jack had bowed like a courtier and then took Angie's hand. Jack held her close as they rocked more than danced to the final slow tune.

Blinking as a teacher switched on the bright lights, Jack kissed her cheek and said he would contact her via WhatsApp.

Back home, Angie told me it was like a dream because everything was so different from her real life. Jack and Angie exchanged WhatsApp messages for a while—mainly about music, but with snippets of their lives. Angie realised that Jack came from a wealthy family and suddenly felt ashamed of her modest home shared with her mum. Worlds apart and with little in common beyond music, their messages fizzled out.

Angie told me it could and should have turned into a beautiful memory, but then she discovered she was pregnant. It took a week before Angie plucked up the courage to tell her mum—who was then immediately furious. *How could you have been so foolish?* she had said but softened when she saw Angie's distress. Her mum told her she could have an abortion and she would help her to arrange it.

That was when the arguments began. Angie's mum kept pushing her to call the clinic, saying things like; *You are too young to have a child; There's not enough money; Don't ruin your life over such a mistake.* But what had made Angie angry was her Mum telling her she was still a child.

Angie simply couldn't go through with an abortion. After days of arguing, and with morning sickness taking hold, Angie packed her bags and moved in with her gran.

Gran told Angie she had to tell Jack; he had a right to know. Angie sobbed. *I should have asked him to use a condom—and I didn't.* Gran had wrapped her arms around her and reassured her it would all be OK. And although Angie started several WhatsApp messages to tell Jack, none were sent.

Angie turned down her university place and took an admin role at a local marketing agency. The work wasn't particularly challenging, but Angie liked the creative buzz in the offices, and work took her mind off the swelling of her belly and everything that it meant.

The months passed, and Angie and her mum reconciled. When the baby was on its way, Gran and her mum stayed with her, encouraging her to breathe and then push. After a long labour, Angie gave birth to a beautiful girl. She named her Katy as a way of remembering Jack.

Gran had a bigger house than her mum's, so it was decided that's where Angie and Katy would stay. Katy kept them both up at night, but Gran had borne the disturbances with grace, and Angie grew used to not having much sleep.

When Katy was eight months old, on a bright autumnal day, Angie placed a blanket on the floor of Gran's lounge. Sunlight streamed through the patio windows, creating perfect lighting to take photos. Every month, Angie took photos of Katy. She would choose the best, have them printed and stick them into an old-fashioned album as her mum had done for her. On this day, Katy was like the model baby, cooing, gurgling and smiling. From having no hair when she was born, Katy now had a thick crop of strawberry blonde hair. Realising how much her daughter now looked like Jack, Angie remembered Gran telling her that Jack had the right to know about Katy.

What happened next, Angie told me, was a moment of madness. She opened Jack's WhatsApp chats and wrote a long message with several photos of Katy attached. Her finger had hovered over the send button for a moment, and then she sent it.

She began admiring Katy's photos again, and then like coming back from a faraway place, she realised the enormity of what she had just done. She wanted to delete the message, but it was too late. Angie saw the two ticks showing it was delivered and read. Beating herself up for being so stupid, she wanted to tell Jack to ignore the message—or say something, but what could she say?

Two weeks passed before Jack replied. When his message popped up in the chat window, she dreaded opening it, scared of Jack's reaction. It wasn't, though, what she expected. Jack said he wanted to meet Katy and would arrange to fly to London to meet his daughter.

Angie's anxiety went into overdrive as she considered why he was doing this. *Was Jack going to demand joint custody? Would Jack's family want to take Katy away from her?* However, Angie agreed that Jack could meet Katy, and they exchanged messages about flights and nearby hotels. Jack didn't give Angie any clue about what he wanted from her or Katy in these messages.

Later that month, at Heathrow, Angie waited at the Arrivals Gate. She held Katy so tightly in her arms that her daughter was squiggling for freedom. As Angie bent down to put Katy into her stroller, she saw Jack coming through the barriers, looking for her. She noticed how handsome he was, and he looked more mature than eighteen months ago. Jack was carrying an expensive-looking holdall in one hand and his guitar in a protective cover in the other. Angie waved, and there was an awkward half-hug greeting. Jack smiled hello to Katy, and she gurgled back at him—their strawberry-blond hair and blue eyes a mirror image of one another.

Jack hailed a taxi outside the terminal, asking the driver to drop Angie off at her gran's before going to his hotel. During the ride, they agreed to meet at a nearby park the next day. Angie had chosen the park because Katy loved the baby swing and the small slide, and she thought it would be a safe space to talk to Jack.

The following day, at the park, Angie and Jack took turns pushing Katy on the swing. Jack said he had been upset that Angie had hidden Katy from him, but seeing his beautiful daughter had changed that. Jack said he, too, had not gone to university. He was working for his Dad's timber yard. The work was OK, but he mostly just wanted to play his guitar.

Katy laughed as Jack pushed her higher on the swing. As they parted, Angie offered to be his guide to see some of London's tourist spots. Leaving Katy with Gran, Angie took Jack to see the Tower of London and the Tate Modern, and they rode on the London Eye. Slowly their polite conversations began to thaw.

At the end of the first week, Angie invited Jack to dinner. Gran hugged Jack as if he was a long-lost family member. She had cooked an embarrassingly large amount of food, which Jack tucked into with gusto. After dinner, Gran had gone into full Spanish Inquisition mode. How long was he staying? Did he have a visa to work here? Did Jack have enough money to keep staying at the hotel? Angie was embarrassed at Gran's directness, but Jack was unruffled and politely answered. Other than a ticket home, he told them he had no plans.

Soon Jack was regularly joining them for dinner. Gran enjoyed Jack's company. For a young man, she told Angie, he knows a lot about politics, art and culture. Jack helped Angie with Katy's night-time routine, and then after dinner, he helped Gran with the dishes before returning to his hotel. Angie felt increasingly comfortable in Jack's company, but it still felt dreamlike. Their relationship, if you could call it that, was going too fast, and she worried about what would happen after Jack returned home.

The next two weeks sped by, and then just days before Jack was due to fly home, he told Angie he wanted to stay in London. Jack asked Angie how she felt about him staying, but when she asked how it would work, he simply reassured her it would all be OK. Swept up in the moment, Angie smiled, which Jack took as a sign of agreement.

In the following weeks, Jack began taking his guitar to Open Mic events. On one of these evenings, he met three guys looking for a lead vocalist for their band. Jack jumped at the chance later telling Angie it was like karma. A few weeks later, Jack invited Angie to meet the band. She liked the funky edge they gave to old Motown classics. Jack's voice was a perfect match for these songs.

Jack moved out of the hotel into a modest bed and breakfast. The band began playing Saturday night gigs—mostly at local pubs. Angie had wondered how he could live on the small amount of cash from these nights—but she was too embarrassed to ask him about it. Jack continued to see Katy and Angie—but not as often as in the beginning. He was always kind to Angie, but he lit up when he played with Katy.

Late in the spring, Gran invited Jack to move into the spare room, telling him he could stay rent-free in exchange for some jobs around the house. And so, Jack had moved in with them. One night after Gran had gone to bed, Angie and Jack opened a bottle of wine. Later, on the stairs, supposedly going up to their separate rooms, Jack turned and kissed Angie. He wished her a good night's sleep, but Angie took his hand and led him into her bedroom. They made love, and this time Angie felt good and dared to dream they would become a family.

Jack became increasingly worried about the gigs—not musically, which he loved—but earning money, which violated his tourist visa. Jack told Angie he wanted to stay in London and asked whether she would consider getting married. It wasn't a down-on-one-knee proposal, and there had not been an ounce of romance in his request. It felt more like he had asked if she could make him a cup of tea. Angie knew Jack liked her, he was a wonderful dad, and Katy loved him. *Was it wrong to marry a man you loved when you knew he didn't love you?* Angie hesitated momentarily, then smiled at Jack and said yes.

Their wedding was at a registry office—not a white wedding that Angie had hoped for, but their first year together had been mostly good. Jack's band were playing at bigger and better-paid gigs. With more money and the help of Gran, they moved out and into their own small flat. Now a toddler, Katy was adorable and loved her Dada. Meanwhile, Angie had been promoted to junior designer.

As the band received more interest, they landed gigs outside of London. Angie knew girls at the gigs drooled over Jack, just as she had once done. For Jack, performing with the band was the most important part of his life, yet Angie knew he enjoyed the adulation too. Sometimes after a gig, Jack didn't come home. He said the boys needed to relax and wind down. She wondered whether Jack was being faithful, and inevitably, memories of how Jack had led her to the storage room sprang to mind. *Had he taken other girls there?* Angie was too scared to ask about the past, or where he stayed when he didn't come home, so she simply accepted Jack's behaviour.

When the band hired a manager, things quickly took off. Their manager helped them produce their first album, and radio stations picked up their music. Jack and Angie laughed and whooped the first time they heard the band's single on air—a song Jack had written. The band manager then lined up interviews on radio shows and helped them up the ladder as a support act to a bigger band. He also wangled an invite to the showcasing artists' stage at the SXSW music festival in Austin.

Angie was excited for Jack and loved the idea of returning to the USA. That is, until Jack said he couldn't afford to pay for all of them to go. He also said he would combine this trip with visiting his family and would be away for a month. Angie told me she felt like Jack was ashamed of her. There had not been a card or a gift from Jack's family to mark their wedding. Jack said they were unhappy with his choice to focus on music instead of helping them with their timber business. It wasn't, he said, anything to do with Angie.

Desperately wanting to reconnect with Jack before his big trip, Angie had asked whether he'd like Katy to have a sibling. Jack's response was instant and adamant. Now wasn't a good time. It was too much pressure now the band were beginning to break through. Angie had silently sighed and didn't bring it up again.

Soon after Jack's return from the USA, Angie noticed that when she walked into the room, Jack would cut phone conversations short or snap his laptop shut. One evening, when Jack was out, she saw he had left his laptop at home. Angie opened the lid, and the screen flickered into life. She typed in Jack's password—the one he used for everything. His Facebook page opened with a chat box showing messages from Mary-Ann. Reading through them, Angie discovered that Mary-Ann had been with Jack at SXSW.

Angie wailed. When Jack returned a few hours later, she flew at him, her arms beating his chest. All the pent-up hurt, sadness and anger exploded in a tirade of awful words. Jack looked aghast, pushed her away, picked up his laptop and walked out.

That happened, Angie told me, six months ago. Jack was still in London and had recently said he didn't want a divorce, claiming he still wanted to see Katy. Angie said she knew that was true, but the bigger truth was his residency in the UK depended on him being married. Jack now gave Angie money to help look after Katy, which she was grateful for, but it also felt like emotional blackmail.

As a final added woe, Angie told me her Gran had recently fallen, breaking her wrist. She was OK, but the plaster cast made everyday chores difficult. Angie didn't wish to burden Gran with her troubles. Angie's Mum had been unsympathetic, telling Angie she needed to grow up. This, she said, was why she decided to come to see me.

Angie's story was like a soap opera—the kind where you can predict the ending from the beginning. But Angie's pain, loss and confusion were real. So, we began working together using EFT to release some of the sadness, hurt and grief of losing a dearly-wished-for relationship that was never really real.

The dim-lit store room is where this story really began. Angie's intuition alerted her that it didn't feel right, yet at that moment, and at times later on, she felt unable to say no. We've all done something like this—agreeing or complying when it intuitively felt wrong.

Angie and Jack's relationship wasn't based on love or even a deep friendship. Without this foundation, they both muddled through trying to do the right thing. No one and no relationship is ever perfect, but healthy relationships need open and honest communication with strong boundaries. Angie and Jack lacked these fundamentals.

Much of my work with Angie was to help her restore boundaries. We identified what was important to her. These new tools would help Angie better define her boundaries in new, future relationships.

Angie and Jack had frequently trampled over their personal boundaries. Some can be easily identified; others are more obscure. Here are the key ones that I spotted.

* The first time they had sex, it was consensual, but neither spoke about or took any form of protection.

* Angie didn't tell Jack about the pregnancy.
* Jack asked Angie to marry him primarily to stay in the UK.
* Angie married Jack when she knew he didn't love her.
* Angie was too afraid to ask Jack where he stayed when he didn't come home.
* Angie breached Jack's privacy by viewing his Facebook page.
* Jack had an affair with Mary-Ann.
* Jack had not asked Angie how she felt about staying married.

DEFINING YOUR BOUNDARY LINES

Defining boundaries and, if necessary, defending them is really about seeing you are worthy and loveable just as you are. You and me—all of us—are magnificent works in progress. Every day we can grow, improve, blossom and then do even more the next day. The process may take a lifetime to master, and we will make mistakes along the way. The secret of success is to learn from life events and choose to do things differently in the future.

Your boundary lines may be relatively easy to identify and action—as Simon's were—or more muddled like they were for Angie. No matter what is going on in your life, begin by looking at your relationships. Who supports you no matter what—like Gran did for Angie? Do some people crush your hopes and dreams? Are there people who constantly say and do things you disagree with—as Dave did to Simon? Do you walk on eggshells with a loved one because you are scared of upsetting them?

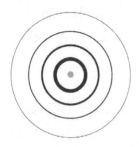

As no two people have precisely the same boundaries, and we are often in the dark about where our boundaries lie, it helps to have a visible structure. I use what looks like an archery target. The dot in the innermost circle, represents you. The radiating circles represent your boundaries.

The innermost circles represent your most important boundaries, while the outer circles have lesser importance. In the exercise below, you will also discover where important people in your life fit into your boundary circles.

WHO IS WHERE?

Begin this exercise by drawing a large bullseye on an A4 sheet of paper, like the one on the previous page. Now identify who is in your inner circle and who populates the others. To do this, intuitively write their initials or name in the circles. The aim is to identify the position of 15–25 people in your life—family members, friends, work colleagues and people you share time with socially.

In the innermost circle, without any boundaries between you and them— who resides there? These will be people you cherish, love and trust. They love and get you just as you are even when you show up as your worst self.

Choose intuitively—not logically. Your inner circle may or may not include parents, children or siblings. An inner circle rarely holds more than a handful of people—sometimes, there are just one or two. Recently, I did this exercise with a client who had no one in her inner circle—not even her husband—which helped her see how much she didn't let anyone get close to her. If you too have no one in your inner circle, please don't beat yourself up—instead, see it as something to work on.

The second circle is typically where you have family members and close friends. You share most of your life with these people but not quite everything. There are more friends in the third and fourth circles, with perhaps some work colleagues and social/sport/faith or activity friends. In the outermost circle, there might be a boss, an ex-partner who is the mother/father of your children, and acquaintances. Again, trust your instincts about who goes where.

Now it's completed, are there any surprises? Have some people edged into your inner circles who should not be there? Or is there someone languishing in an outer circle who you wish was closer? Make a note of any changes you would like. This awareness in itself will begin to change things.

NOTICING BOUNDARY CROSSINGS

All boundary crossings stimulate a substantial, adverse emotional response. Bring to mind an occasion where you felt you were treated unkindly, unfairly or were made to feel uncomfortable. What *exactly* did they say or do? Was it their words that got under your skin? Or their tone of voice? Or was it what they did? Now ask yourself, Do I always react like this? Or is it just when this person says or does that to me?'

Make some notes about who or what is pushing your buttons.

BEGIN USING THE TECHNIQUE OF 'NO ONE MAY...'

Take a pen and write 'No one may...' then complete the sentence with whatever comes to mind. Writing it down will help you connect to a deeper place within yourself. It's OK to write anything. Don't judge yourself—this is just to unblock the things you edit out due to social niceties. This constructed sentence isn't going to be said to anyone. Writing *no one may* sentences simply helps you to identify your boundaries without confining them to just one person. And yet, at the same time, one person may instantly spring to mind. Let me give you a few common examples:

'No one may be disrespectful to me at work.'
'No one may keep asking me to do more than my fair share of the household chores.'
'No one may tell me I'm stupid.'

Now write three or four sentences for yourself, each beginning with *no one may...* Who or what has recently irked, infuriated or made you feel angry? The act of writing it down can, surprisingly, already release some of the power this holds over you.

Now it's time to consider whether or not you should speak to the person or people in question.

CHOOSING WHETHER OR NOT TO DEFINE A BOUNDARY

Every day we cross someone's boundaries—just as much as they cross ours. Rarely is it done maliciously; rather, it is often done thoughtlessly, not realising their boundaries are different from ours.

Reviewing your *no one may...* sentences, which one troubles you the most? Who is crossing this boundary? Now consider, was it a one-off—were they perhaps having a bad day? Or do they say/do this regularly?

When choosing which boundaries to tackle, there is a balance to be struck. To a degree, we need not let their words or behaviour ruffle our feathers, but at the same time it is not OK for someone to persistently treat you in a way that you feel is wrong. Nor should a serious one-off infringement necessarily pass without comment. Trust your intuition about standing up for what you think is right and when to let it go.

What though, if it is fear holding you back? Fear is a natural instinct designed to keep us safe—yet fear can become warped, and what we think we are afraid of might not be real. In other words, the consequence of standing up for yourself may bring about the total opposite outcome of the one you had feared.

Putting boundaries back in place can take more than an ounce of courage. In the next chapter, I'll show you how to define and defend your boundaries using Truth Talking.

Truth Talking—
the graceful art of saying *No*

We need to find the courage to say no to the things and people
that are not serving us if we want to rediscover ourselves
and live our lives with authenticity.

♥ Barbara De Angelis

Do you ever wish you could re-run a conversation? Like the one where, with cheeks flushed, your words were shot like arrows—aimed to hurt. Or maybe the time you felt bamboozled, and it was only afterwards that you thought of all the smart and witty things you *could* have said. We've all had conversations like this. Truth Talking is a method that can help you put these times right—even weeks after the event.

WHAT IS TRUTH TALKING?

Truth Talking helps people have difficult conversations in a dignified way. The method includes using I-Statements, and it evolved during role-playing with my clients. Armed with words provided by my client, I would take on the role of their partner, boss, colleague or family member. In this safe space, clients could practice and witness what it was like to speak their truth—as Simon had done with Dave.

When what is felt is not spoken about, it often leads to walking on eggshells, which is exhausting. Fear of telling others how we feel about their words and actions may make us defensive. Our sentences in both situations become littered with the word you, especially when *you* is emphasised. For example, saying phrases like, **You** *always...* or *Why do* **you** *have to...* or *Don't* **you** *see that...*

In the early days of working with my clients facing such difficulties, I simply encouraged them to switch their sentence structure from using *you* to *I*. Then to make their tone of voice as neutral as possible. Doing this alone often makes challenging conversations easier and produces better outcomes.

Over time, Truth Talking developed into a simple three-step formula to help the other person hear what was being said. You might assume that this is already the case, yet when someone is in their own world or triggered, it's surprising how much the other person misses. Truth Talking can help you draw a line in the sand and stop cycling arguments tearing you and the other person apart. It can also bring about new, creative solutions. But perhaps its greatest strength is to help you nail your feelings about what is happening.

Alesha's story below shows how resolving even a tiny issue can make life easier.

ALESHA'S STORY

At the beginning of my life coaching career, I did much of my work on the phone. The anonymity of telephone coaching is more powerful than might be imagined. Clients can share their secrets without seeing my face. And as their Life Coach, I can hone in on the words and vocal energy. Surprisingly, this is equally revealing as working with someone face-to-face. The tone of voice, cadence, word emphasis, repetitions of keywords, hesitations and how quickly someone talks speaks volumes about what is going on for that person.

Alesha was a telephone client. She didn't live locally to me, but if we had passed in the street, I would not have recognised her—unless, of course, she spoke to me. Sometimes I meet past telephone clients—at talks, workshops or shows—and they always look different from expected. It's not that I consciously create a picture of these clients, and yet seeing them in person, requires putting a face to a voice I know so well. So, I didn't know what Alesha looked like or how old she was, but I came to know her very well. Alesha was intelligent, quick-witted and determined to make her life better. I also loved that she saw the funny side of life, often making me laugh.

Alesha was a partner in a business going through a tough patch. She was also a single mum with a teenage daughter. And on top of this, her new boyfriend was inconsiderate and unkind. Our sessions were primarily to resolve her work and love-life issues. However, at the beginning of one of our telephone sessions, Alesha shared with me that her daughter, Sienna, was driving her crazy.

Sienna, I found out, loved taking baths. Alesha told me she was happy that Sienna used this as a way of relaxing—especially with exams looming. However, after bathing, Sienna would leave the water in the bath with several damp towels on the floor.

I asked Alesha how she was dealing with this. She replied, 'I keep asking Sienna not to do this, but she ignores me. Yesterday, I was angry and shouted, *For goodness sake—is it too much to ask for **you** to pull the plug? I have enough on my plate without tidying up after **you**!* With a sigh, she added, 'And I still had to pick up her towels.'

Alesha shared she knew it was ridiculous and it shouldn't bother her, but the plug chain was broken, and she hated putting her hand in the cold soapy water. She thought Sienna might be doing it on purpose—to wind her up.

I heard Alesha sigh on the call, and I sensed this was draining her energy. So, I suggested the possibility that Sienna wasn't listening, and if she did, this might change things. Alesha was intrigued and agreed to explore this further.

After explaining the Truth Talking technique, we began constructing the three slightly unnatural sentences. The first sentence was to genuinely acknowledge Sienna for who she was and what she was doing. The second would be Alesha's emotional statement—how she felt about the cold bath water and wet towels. And finally, the third sentence would be a curiosity question to ask why it was happening.

After a few trials, Alesha decided her three sentences would be,

'I know you enjoy taking a bath because it helps you relax after studying.'

'I feel taken for granted when the bath is left full of cold, soapy water and the towels are left on the floor.'

'I was wondering why this happens?'

We role-played the words—especially eliminating the desire to say *but* before the second sentence. During our role-play, I played a petulant Sienna, and Alesha practised keeping her voice calm.

Alesha was still sceptical. She asked, 'Why will Sienna listen now—when she didn't before?'

I replied, 'Because she is far more likely to hear you.'

I quickly added, 'I know this way of speaking feels odd, but how would it be if Sienna stopped doing this?'

'It would be amazing.'

'OK—then I would love for you to give it go.'

Alesha agreed and told me she would speak with Sienna after school—while it was still fresh in her mind.

On Alesha's next coaching session, she gushed, 'You will never believe what happened with Sienna. I did it exactly as we had practised, and guess what she said?'

I ventured, 'From your voice—it sounds good?'

'Sienna said, *Oh—do I do that? Sorry Mum—I'll try to remember*. Can you believe that!'

I laughed—I could believe it.

'So, Guru Jennie,' Alesha teased, 'tell me why it worked?'

'Mostly, it's just Sienna being a typical teenager and not listening to you. Speaking to Sienna after discovering the left-in bath water would have given your voice an edge. Teenagers are highly tuned-in to vocal energy when there is even a hint of *you-are-in-trouble*. Because you were upset with Sienna, there was a tendency to use *you* rather than *I*, which Sienna would have picked up, so she switched off.'

I could hear Alesha's smile coming down the phone when she asked, 'Hmm, interesting. Do you think this approach will work for my work colleagues?'

And so, we began working on the next piece of her jigsaw puzzle in putting boundaries back in place at work.

WILL THIS TECHNIQUE ALWAYS WORK?

No—not always. With Sienna, Truth Talking worked beautifully. But many teenagers are naturally rebellious as they pull away from their parents to discover their own path. The teenage years can be challenging! However, even with teenagers, this approach has far more chance of succeeding than a conversation that contains an accusatory *you*. When using Truth Talking with an adult, it has a high success rate for resolving tricky situations or dilemmas.

TRUTH TALKING METHOD

Truth Talking begins with three sentences constructed before a conversation takes place. Working out what needs to be said, writing it down and practising it means that in the moment, there is a greater possibility of you following your intention.

Creating a Genuine Acknowledgement. So often, people do not want to acknowledge the other person. They are angry—no way do they want to say anything nice to the other person. Instead, they want to request or demand change. And yet, the Genuine Acknowledgement is vital. When you share that you understand what is going on for the person you are about to speak to, they will more readily listen to what you have to say. What you say must be genuine, as false compliments will backfire.

To begin, ask yourself what you know to be true about the other person. Who are they? What was going on for them when they said or did the thing that upset you? Alesha's Genuine Acknowledgement to Sienna was, *I know you enjoy taking a bath because it helps you relax after studying.* For Simon, it was, *I know that the reason you call me Miller is the other Simon is our boss.* Here are a few more examples that you can adapt and use.

> 'I understand the deadline is next week. As a team leader, I know much
> of the responsibility for hitting our target falls on your shoulders.'
> 'I know how hard you have worked, so we can afford a holiday.'
> 'I can see how stressful it is, dealing with your Dad's illness on top
> of everything else.'
> 'I know you are a good dad and want the best for our children.'
> 'I respect your religious beliefs and know how important they are
> to you.'

Putting together an Emotional Statement. People also hesitate when I ask them to tell the other person how they feel. They fear that showing vulnerability will lead to the other person taking advantage of them. Yet this is rarely the case.

To see this, imagine the situation was the other way around, if someone calmly expressed how your words or behaviour had caused distress. Would your first thought be to take advantage of them? No. Most people will consider what has been said and most likely make changes after the conversation. Of course, a tiny minority of people like Dave in Simon's story won't want to play ball.

When someone actively chooses to rebel, they nearly always carry pain inside. I suspect Dave was jealous of Simon, which was probably the root cause of why he initially continued to call Simon by his surname.

For the Emotional Statement, you share your feelings about what they said or did—and the impact this has had. Whatever you feel—angry, hurt, sad, infuriated—is said calmly and with respect. In particular, without an accusation such as—*you did this to me*. Sharing what is felt creates an opportunity for healing and new solutions.

It is natural to want to accuse the other person when we believe it's all down to their wrong-doing—yet blaming isn't helpful. This desire to point the finger at the other person is a defence mechanism to keep us safe. In reality, our emotions are triggered by the situation, our past experiences and how we feel in the moment. It's never totally about what the other person has said or done. One day we may all be enlightened souls, and the words and actions of others will be like water off a duck's back. Until then, we will sometimes react because we can't see another way of handling the situation. Truth Talking allows us to honour our feelings and find ways to put things right.

Most Emotional Statements begin with *I am...* or *I feel...* When the other person hears an accurate account of what we felt, they pay more attention because our energy and words align.

Nailing the emotion for the Emotional Statement can be tricky. The list of emotions in the chapter, *Become Emotionally Savvy,* may be helpful. That list is by no means complete—there are many hundreds of names for our feelings. Using your expressions is totally OK as long as they are respectful.

Here are a few examples of Emotional Statements.

> 'I am hurt that everything was arranged without asking me what I
> thought about it.'
> 'I feel angry that my mother was dismissed as being boring.'
> 'I feel unloved and unappreciated for all the cooking and cleaning
> I do.'
> 'I feel scared when there is so much anger between us.'
> 'I am nervous about taking on this new job as I have received
> insufficient training.'

It can be challenging to craft non-personal sentences like those above. We desperately want to drop *you* back into the sentence. For example, I *felt angry when **you** said my mother was boring*. Stressing the **you** makes your sentence personal, which changes the tone and, therefore, the likely response. Truth Talking isn't a natural way of speaking, so it helps to write down your sentence and craft it until you have something that works.

Make a request, or Step into Wonderland. For the final sentence, there is a choice. It is either a straightforward request or an invitation to help find a solution agreeable for you. Your preference will depend on the relationship. Requests such as, *I would like...* or even, *I need...*, may feel easier and give you more control. And, often such requests are honoured. However, there may be less buy-in from the person you are talking to, and the request may be forgotten out of habit, as the bookkeeper did in Simon's story. Whenever possible, I recommend using the Step into Wonderland approach, as this finds better solutions. These sentences begin with,

'I am curious about how...'

or

'I am wondering how...'

Make sure this sentence is genuinely curious. Sentences such as, *I'm wondering if you could do the food shopping on Saturday mornings?* is simply a polite request. The Wonderland approach would be, *I'm wondering how we could better organise the food shopping?*

Before putting this into action, there are a few more considerations.

GETTING COMFORTABLE USING I

Very young children's language is often full of *I want...* and *I don't want...* to ask for, make demands and refuse to do what has been requested. Even at this tender age, they are learning the art of negotiation. Parents usually correct their children's demands with something like:

'Angel, it's not, *I want*. It is, please may I have.'

Teaching our children to be polite is, of course, good. However, around the age of twelve, with a more comprehensive understanding of language, tone and nuance, children could be taught how to use *I* assertively. Unfortunately, this rarely happens, which can lead to feeling uncomfortable with sentences beginning with *I*. Yet using *I* in a neutral tone simply expresses a point of view, not superiority.

UNDERSTANDING WHY USING YOU CAN BACKFIRE

Some people easily start sentences with *I*, while others avoid it altogether. Some people use *you* a lot, and a few opt for the royal *we*—even when talking about themselves. We mainly use these pronouns the same way our parents used them. So, starting sentences with *I* may come naturally— or it could be challenging.

No matter how we typically use pronouns, as soon as someone ruffles our feathers, our sentence structure changes. Tell-tale signs show in the more frequent use of *you* as we subconsciously separate ourselves from the other person. And our tone of voice becomes harsher.

When we hear an emphasised *you*, the most common reaction is to see it as a threat. This can happen even though it may have been nothing more than a poor choice of words with negative nuance. Our reaction is due to our subconscious initiating the fight or flight response. In survival mode, our body instigates immediate biological changes to process information faster. These changes include muting the slower rational, analytical part of the brain, giving preference to the lightning-fast part of the brain to react instinctively.

While our brain is in survival mode, we don't fully hear what was said or intended. Rather, we focus more on vocal tone and body language to assess whether or not it is safe. When our survival mode dissipates, we may realise what was said or meant. These changes are also why, in a heated discussion, finding the right words to say is hard because we have less access to rational thought. And it's why all the great things we wanted to say flood into our minds when we are calm again.

To get a feeling for how this works, read the following statements—aloud if possible. Add emphasis to the word *you*, to hear how accusatory and blaming these words sound.

'Why didn't **you** finish it today—**you** knew there was a deadline!'
'**You** are always letting me down!'
'**You** don't care about me—it's always what **you** want.'
'**You** can't keep doing this to me!'
'Why do **you** always do that?'

Did one of these sentences, in particular, make you feel uncomfortable, even though these sentences have no context? It's fascinating to notice how easily we are triggered. Our subconscious remembers past hurtful comments and frequently reacts similarly to earlier events.

When a difficult conversation is needed, using *I* instead of *you*, means you are less likely to trigger the other person's survival responses.

PUTTING TRUTH TALKING INTO PRACTICE

Are you ready to try your first Truth Talking conversation? Perhaps while reading this, you have someone in mind who has recently crossed a line? Tackling things that have gotten under our skin may be too scary for the first attempt. So, put that issue to one side, and choose an easier target for practice.

If you have young children or teenagers, this provides endless opportunities to practice Truth Talking. A few ideas could be encouraging children to tidy their bedroom, prepare their school bags the night before, or play more kindly with their siblings. With young children, still use *I* and not *you*, but make the sentences less formal and in keeping with their level of understanding.

Alternatively, it could be a minor infringement at work or with a family member. Stumped as to who you could practice this on or what you wish to improve? Take another look at your *No-one may...* sentences that you formulated in the last chapter.

After crafting your three sentences, how do you now feel about having this conversation? Consider the likely outcomes of saying these words versus staying silent. Sometimes, just working things out shows you what needs to change on your side—and that may be enough. However, if the desire to put things right is still strong, and any consequences are better than not speaking up, give it go.

IF TIME HAS ELAPSED SINCE THE EVENT

For situations that happened a while ago, you may need a simple reminder before launching into Truth Talking. You don't need to tell the whole story. Rather you just need to set the scene. Here are a few examples:

> 'Last night when we talked about our holiday—I would like to go back to that.'
>
> 'At last month's Sales Meeting, we spoke about the budget. It has been bothering me, and I'd like to discuss it again.'
>
> 'At Diana's birthday party, there was a lot of teasing. I'd like to share my thoughts about this.'

When the person indicates that they remember the time you are referring to, then start with your pre-worked-out sentences.

CREATING AN EXIT STRATEGY

When attempting a new way of doing anything, it might go pear-shaped. The other person's responses may trigger you despite working out what you wish to say. Or you may catch yourself being defensive, using *you* instead of *I*, or even just feeling flustered. So, just in case you need it, prepare an exit strategy—a few words to make a quick exit. Here are a few examples.

> 'Sorry, I'm not handling this well. I'm going for a walk. I still want to talk about this—just not now.'
>
> 'I just needed for you to hear this. Please think about it—then we can talk again soon.'
>
> 'I'd like to ask that we press the pause button and return to this later.'

When our first attempt at Truth Talking doesn't go well, this is not failing—rather it is learning. Simply allow time for your survival response to diminish, then, in an hour or two, or the next day—but not much longer than that—try again. In times like this, I remember Paulo Cohelo's quote, *Success comes from falling down seven times, but getting back up eight times.*

I trust you will not have to do seven rounds! Yet it may take more than one attempt to achieve your desired result. When you have completed this, you will feel better and have the tools to apply it to future situations.

WHAT HAPPENS NEXT?

What happens next will depend on the urgency, difficulty or ease of the subject you have chosen to tackle. Sometimes Truth Talking leads to instant results or stimulates a good conversation. Sometimes the other person is surprised at your new approach—so it's best to leave them to think about what you have said.

FINAL CONSIDERATIONS FOR TRUTH TALKING

When coaching Alesha, I asked her to speak her three sentences calmly. It's not just our words that convey our messages. Our body language and the emotional charge in our voice tell the other person far more than we might imagine. The emphasis of certain words, especially *I* or *you*, can change the meaning. For example, saying *I hate you* in a soft, gooey voice doesn't convey hatred. And saying *I love you* in a disapproving tone doesn't sound like love either.

To keep your vocal tone neutral, imagine the sound of your voice draws a line that looks like the rolling hills of England. In this way, your voice comes across as pleasant and non-threatening. When we're angry or hurt, our voice may sound like falling off the cliff edge at Dover!

Be an observer when delivering your Genuine Acknowledgement. Did you notice the other person subconsciously nodding their head to your words? Witnessing this is a good sign that they are interested in what you are about to say. No matter what, remember you are worthy of your values, dreams and beliefs. Standing up for what is important to you isn't always easy, but with Truth Talking, you now have new tools to change relationships for the better.

Humiliation, shame and the dungeon of your soul

Every experience,
no matter how bad it seems,
holds within a blessing of some kind.
The goal is to find it.
♥ Buddha

Moments after any humiliating event, shame and embarrassment flare up. Feelings of being mortified, belittled or threatened are common too. Afterwards, you may be angry and have a burning desire to put the record straight, especially if the allegations were false.

Occasionally, humiliation may lead to confusion, especially if the words or actions come from someone close. *How could they have done that? Why didn't they see how hurtful that was?* If belittling happens in an intimate relationship and it becomes frequent, it will tear the relationship apart. Or, sadly, it may become a pattern of coercive control, eroding the self-esteem of the one on the receiving end.

Mostly, we experience humiliation when someone in a powerful position shames us while others witness the event. Yet we may also experience humiliation in more subtle ways. For example, when we don't receive a salary increase yet we know others doing similar work have been rewarded. Or a group of our supposedly good friends keep us out of the loop. Then, what appears to be accidentally revealed, we hear about what the rest of the group have said, agreed or done in our absence.

In all these events, no matter what was said, implied or done, humiliation can scar the psyche, and we rarely forget what happened. Even decades later, the recollection remains crystal clear. These events are kept alive to provide tools and coping mechanisms for similar events in the future. However, holding on to anger, hatred or the desire for revenge is ultimately more painful than finding a way to be at peace with what transpired. Letting go isn't about forgetting what happened—that won't work—but there are ways for it reside in the background so it is no longer a trigger. Before going deeper into processing and handling humiliation, I'd like to share an experience I carried around for decades.

MY STORY: SHAME AND HATRED

Mr Brown was my first music teacher at secondary school. I think he was Scottish. There was a distinctive lilt to his voice, but he was not a cheerful man. His grey hair and eyes matched his steely determination to educate us in all things musical.

In the corner of the music room stood Mr Brown's pride and joy—a small gramophone. He began our lessons by playing classical music from one of his beloved LPs. Close your eyes, he instructed, and listen. What emotions, he would ask, is the composer conveying?

With my eyes closed, I drifted off to another world where I listened to my favourite music on Radio Caroline and my dad's Beatles records. By contrast, Mr Brown's musical choices sounded sombre and dreary to my young ears.

After listening to classical music, it would be time to play musical instruments. On this day, Mr Brown handed out an assortment of recorders, triangles, xylophones, tambourines and melodicas. He asked us to move our chairs into small groups—according to the instruments in our hands—like a simple orchestra. I had the dreaded melodica. This strange instrument looks like an oversized, flattened recorder with piano-like keys instead of holes.

On the blackboard, Mr Brown had chalked a simple tune, indicating the different parts we were to play. Each group practised a few times, and then, baton in hand, Mr Brown conducted us to play together. The contrast between the listened-to music and our cacophony was awful. And in part, I was responsible.

As we played, I looked at the blackboard, gazed down to see which finger I should press, and then blew into the melodica. My eyes flickered between the blackboard and my fingers. I knew I was supposed to keep my eyes on the music and instinctively know which finger to press and blow, but I didn't trust myself. Realising I was behind my classmates—I jumped a note.

Mr Brown raised his arms and shouted 'Stop'. Slowly he walked from the front of the classroom to the back of my chair. Standing behind me, he cupped my ears with his hands and rubbed them hard. Then he yelled, 'You're not listening to the tune—read the music, girl!'

His raised voice silenced my classmates. I could feel my cheeks burning, and I bit my tongue to stop tears from welling up. Everyone was looking at me. Some, I sensed, were glad it wasn't them taking the flak.

'Let's begin again, and this time stay in tune!'

I picked up the melodica and placed it to my lips. I continued to look at the notes and moved my fingers, but I didn't blow. I prayed Mr Brown would not notice one melodica was not making a sound.

From that moment, I hated Mr Brown and his music lessons. As a consequence, I didn't master reading music or learn to play a musical instrument—which I now regret.

It makes me feel so old to say this, but I think this proviso is important. When I was eleven, it was not uncommon for kids, mostly boys, to receive physical punishment from teachers. It was rare, but I remember a boy in my class being canned while we were made to watch. Not paying attention in class could lead to holding heavy books in outstretched arms. When arms tired, the teacher would sharply tap your hands with a ruler to keep them up. So, although Mr Brown's ear-rubbing was harsh for a musically clumsy child, it was not an exceptional punishment.

PROCESSING AN HUMILIATING EVENT

I did with Mr Brown what most people do after a humiliating event—I demonised, hated and blamed him. Most people will similarly find ways to shun or avoid the person who hurt them. Shortly after such an incident, the mind usually re-runs the event, considering all the brilliant things that could or should have been said to counter the putdowns. However, often that is as far as it goes. The power dynamic in humiliation is usually unequal. A teacher can ignore the voice or rights of a student. A boss is more powerful than an employee, and a parent has dominance over a young child. But not dealing with the impact of humiliation—healing and letting it go—leaves us stuck. To begin the healing process of humiliation, we first need to look at its common emotional partner—shame.

THE PURPOSE OF HEALTHY SHAME

At one time or another, we have all betrayed our moral guidance—betraying treasured values and beliefs. We may have stepped across our line because we were pushed, exhausted or stressed. Sometimes we may have chosen to do these things out of spite or for one-upmanship or devilment. No one leads a perfect life—even attempting this would quickly become unbearable. So, at times, for all kinds of reasons, our imperfect self will do and say things that we know are wrong. Afterwards, we may deny what we did, or start praying to get away with it, or fool ourselves that it was OK to have done or said those things. Yet when we have crossed a significant line, healthy shame will gnaw at our soul until the day we admit to what we have done. This is shame's primary purpose—to act as a messenger to help us get back on track.

Sadly, we are living in a world where feelings of shame are considered bad. So, even knowing we have done wrong, and even if caught out, there is a strong tendency to push shame away. We fight against it even when the body is in full alarm mode with cheeks flushed red, tears welling in our eyes, and legs that have turned to jelly. Our societal programming considers shame as threatening. And so, we rarely listen to the messages that shame brings, which could help us put things right.

Putting things right, of course, is seldom easy or straightforward. A classic example of this shows up in affairs. On the first occasion of crossing a line—an inappropriate text, a kiss, or sex—feelings of shame flood the psyche. But it's never just feelings of shame. Depending on the state of the primary relationship, the secrecy may feel like falling in love all over again. Or it may bring up confusion and disbelief at what has been allowed. With those feelings, paralysing dread often leads to being ostrich-like and burying the head in the sand.

Affairs seldom start intentionally. Instead, they begin because a need isn't being met within themselves or an expectation in the primary relationship has not been fulfilled. Often the one having an affair is not looking to have their cake and eat it. Rather, once it has started, they don't know how to extricate themselves. Shame brings messages of owning up to what has happened, remorse, sorrow, and guidance to ask for forgiveness. Yet the fear of hurting the two people they like, love or admire feels impossible to resolve. It is easy to think people would not continue an affair with such thoughts. Yet, affairs are complex, and such behaviour is commonplace. Most often, affairs are discovered by a ticket, a text message or a credit card statement that doesn't add up. Being found out is often a relief to the one having an affair. Few people can lead a duplicitous double life.

HOW TO PROCESS AND HEAL SHAMING

Healthy shame arises naturally in reaction to our wrongdoing to help us restore our values as to what is and isn't OK. Humiliation, by contrast, is most often a public shaming. In medieval times, people were locked into stocks as a punishment for minor offences. With their feet shackled, local people pelted them with rotten food. Thankfully we no longer do that, but humiliation conducted in a public space often has a similar intent. The person belittling another wants their victim to be seen as not good enough.

For some people, being shamed in public can lead to feelings of stigmatisation, isolation and hopelessness. For others, it ignites intense rage to put things right. How you deal with humiliation depends mainly on your relationship with that other person, your personality type and the depth of the attack on your values.

A child who is humiliated to the point of not feeling good enough, may, as an adult, accept shame even when they know it is unjustified, because it's familiar to them. This acceptance can easily cause a tailspin in self-worth. By contrast, similar words or actions will have far less impact on someone with higher self-esteem. For these people, being shown up may feel uncomfortable, but they are more likely to address what happened or quickly brush it aside.

Whether your self-esteem is low or high, remember one person's view of you is not the view of everyone else. Know this simple truth—in life, you are always at a place of choice. You can believe what was said or dismiss it. You may see some truth in the allegations and, on reflection, choose to make some changes. But the best choice in such circumstances is to see and feel you are still worthy, even if you made a mistake. With this mindset, there is an opportunity to learn, grow and blossom further.

Choosing to honour who you are doesn't instantly change the situation. However, it begins changing your perception of what happened, which helps you get through it.

In Brené Brown's excellent book, *The Gifts of Imperfection—Let Go of Who You Think You're Supposed to Be and Embrace Who You Are*, she speaks eloquently about how shame loves secrecy, and while it hangs out in the shadows, it retains power over you. So, choose to tell someone about what happened. Confide in a good friend. Make sure it's not someone who will advise you to forget about it or, in response, immediately tell you their story which will be bigger, worse or better than yours. Instead, find a compassionate, empathic soul who accepts you for who you are and can listen without judgement. In the sharing, what to do next will often bubble up from deep inside of you.

The secret of dealing with humiliation is not to let it fester. Talking about what happened releases humiliation's power over you. From there, you can begin to reflect on how to turn it around. This process is not always easy—yet you have more power than you might imagine. You are worthy of being treated honourably by everyone.

THE DUNGEON OF THE SOUL

Deep within your soul is place rarely visited—your dungeon. It's where you imprison everyone who has hurt, abused or humiliated you. Long after the event, their energy is still trapped inside your being, and holding on it is rarely helpful.

The following exercise will show you who lives on in your dungeon. It doesn't take long, and you may be surprised by what it reveals. Begin by sitting comfortably, somewhere quiet. Close your eyes. Breathe slowly and deeply for a count of ten, to calm your mind and body. Now, in your mind's eye, prepare to visit your dungeon. Push aside any feelings that this feels silly and let your imagination act as your guide.

See yourself standing inside the thick stone walls of a castle. It may appear as a castle you have visited or one conjured by your imagination.

It doesn't matter what image shows up—trust what you are seeing is the right scene for you. As you look around, notice you are in the middle of a large central courtyard. One of the far corners catches your eye where there is a short flight of stone steps leading down to a heavy, metal-studded door.

Intuitively, you sense this is the way to your dungeon. Go over to the steps, walk down, then open the door. Once inside, see a wide corridor with a vaulted ceiling and a row of burning torches on the walls. Walk along the passageway which takes you further underground. At the far end, the space widens into a room. Thick metal bars, with a metal gate in the middle partitions the room. Behind the bars, are where you keep souls you have trapped there for harming you.

On your side of the room, see a hook holding a large old-fashioned key. This, you sense, opens the gate. Who have you locked inside your dungeon? Make a note of everyone you can see.

REVIEWING THOSE IN YOUR DUNGEON

The first time I did this exercise, I had already forgiven my granddad. Had it been before, I'm sure his presence would have filled the room. So, I was surprised to find a crowd lingering in my dungeon. My ex-husband was there, with a couple of ex-boyfriends, each appearing at the age when I had last known them. Within the group, I saw a young girl, her face hidden in the shadows yet instantly recognisable as Susan. A lady I knew as Grand-Mère was visible too, and at the back stood Mr Brown.

Long ago, all these people had said or done things that made me feel sad, afraid, angry or hurt. Looking at these people now, it felt ridiculous that I was still holding on to their energy. Nonetheless, I needed to consider why I still held on to their words or actions. Perhaps there were lessons that I had not spotted at the time. I also needed to check in with my shadow-self—had

I played a part in what had happened too? Completing this process would allow me to forgive everyone and let them go.

The presence of my ex-husband was the most unexpected. We had divorced with dignity more than twenty years earlier, and today, loosely, we are friends. Considering why he was here, I noticed a lingering sadness for our failed marriage. I recalled how he had not fought for me, and then my shadow-self showed me that I had pushed him away too.

Susan was a tiny fireball of spite from my early childhood. Even though I was taller than her by more than four inches, one day in the playground, she had knocked me over and pulled my hair. A kind dinner lady took me to the school kitchen to wash my bloodied knees and hugged me, but precisely what led to this event is lost in the mists of time.

Grand-Mére is not a relative, she was American and grandmother to Louis and Sylvie, who were my charges when I was a nanny. At eighteen, I was so excited to go to Paris to look after these young tots, but first, I was to travel to Normandy. I was to stay with Grand-Mére to help look after nine-month-old Louis for two weeks, while his parents were in Brazil. She met me at the train station, and hardly said a word to me during the short drive to her home. The two weeks came and went and finally stretched into six. During this time, Grand-Mére wore a constant expression of displeasure whenever I was around. She did her best to ignore me and was impolite. I never figured out why she treated me like this. Perhaps she was aggrieved with her daughter for leaving Louis with her, and then me, a stranger, living in her home.

TIME FOR MR BROWN TO GO

Mr Brown wasn't the first person I released from my dungeon, nor was he the most important. But let me share with you the process I used to forgive and let him go, as it may help you let go of those lingering in your dungeon.

I brought Mr Brown into my mind, seeing him as I had known him at school. He wore a nondescript grey suit, which matched his grey eyes and limp grey hair. *Was he really this grey*? I ignored my thoughts about his appearance and became curious. Did I still hate him? No—it was far too long ago. After that class, I wondered, did he regret cupping my ears and rubbing them? Why had he picked on me? Did he rub the ears of other kids in their music lessons when he was annoyed? Was it down to me daydreaming as well as being out of tune on the day he lost his rag?

Before allowing Mr Brown to go, I knew it was important to look at my shadow-self and see if I had done something similar. It's challenging to see yourself not in your best light. Surely, though, I had not behaved this badly to anyone? Then, from the depths of my soul, a memory surfaced.

In the early days of my graphic design business, I worked alone on the dining room table. Slowly, as my business grew, I took on employees and bigger office spaces. Our last office was a beautiful space with an open plan room with four large, curved desks. And at the far end, my separate office.

Around a year after moving into this office space, I employed a new junior designer, John—a university graduate with a promising portfolio. However, soon I was doubting my judgement. Daily, John arrived late but then left punctually at 5.30 pm. The leaving time was as per his contract, but it bugged me that he left on time despite arriving late. This particularly so when my team and I stayed late to meet a tight deadline. I was also irked by the number of typographical mistakes in John's work. On spotting these, I asked him to come into my office. I would close the door, point out the errors, give him proofreading tips, and urge him to be more careful.

Little things, like the incorrect spelling of a town or name, would ruin a client's brochure, no matter how beautifully it was designed.

John had only worked for me for a short time when one day I received a call from the printers. They were about to print several thousand brochures. They had spotted an error on the films from a job John had produced.

Should they halt the print run? I thanked them for their sharp eyes and promised they would receive new films later that day. I put the phone down and stormed over to John's desk. In my hand, I held a printout of his mistake. I shook the paper in front of him.

'Look at this', I yelled. 'Why didn't you double-check your work? Or ask one of us to look over it? How many more times do I have to tell you to be careful and check everything?'

Steaming, I marched back to my office and slammed the door behind me.

In front of my team, I had humiliated John and made him feel small—just as Mr Brown had done to me. The truth was that I should have spotted that mistake before the films went to the printers. For graphic designers, typographical errors are a constant nightmare. When working on a design project, you begin to read what you think is there—not what really is there. Minor errors like this are so easy to miss. On that day, I didn't spot John's error—but I blamed him for not checking his work when the responsibility was mine.

Recalling how I treated John made me see Mr Brown in a new light. I began to wonder what was going on in his life the day he rubbed my ears. Was he sad or stressed? Had he argued with a loved one? Was he later regretful—as I had been with John? Did he wish to put it right—but didn't know how to do this? Or did he believe this to be an appropriate punishment for me? I will never know. However, recognising how I had similarly humiliated John allowed me to forgive Mr Brown, and I visualised him walking out of my dungeon.

LETTING YOUR PRISONERS GO

Reviewing the list of souls in your dungeon, can you instantly open the gate to liberate some of them? Time is a great healer. Sometimes just recognising those whose energy you have held on to, is enough. Yet there will be others who you hesitate or even refuse to release. This is OK. It's rare to be able to forgive all of your prisoners go in one fell swoop.

For each person you are ready to free, recall what happened, then consider the following. Were there any extenuating circumstances for their poor behaviour? And how has holding on to the emotions connected to the humiliation helped you? The last question is tricky. Immediately, you will want to answer that it hasn't helped. Yet there are always benefits to what we hold on to—even if they are contrary, such as choosing to remember an event with fine detail to prove to others that you were badly treated.

Finally, ask yourself what it would take for you to forgive and let them go. You may need to dig deep into your shadow-self to see your role in what happened. Or find a day when your less-than-best self did something similar. Seeing yourself in their shoes increases your capacity for compassion.

Please don't dwell on memories where you were less than your best. Remember, you and me—all of us—have humiliated someone else at least once in life. No one is perfect—we all sometimes get things wrong. With this in mind, who will you release today?

Masks and revealing your authentic self

We are constantly invited to be who we are.

♥ Henry David Thoreau

In the aftermath of my ex-husband's return to Japan, my inner world fell apart, and I unwittingly, adopted a superwoman mask to cope. Just like Clark Kent, I wore this mask to allow me to be someone else. The mask hid my pain and allowed me to channel my energy into a whirlwind of achievements. During the first year, with my superwoman mask firmly in place, I flew into action.

* I started a graphic design business with no formal design or business experience.
* The PTA at my children's school needed volunteers, so I raised my hand, joined the group, and took on an active role.
* In our new home, I steamed off rolls of painted anaglypta wallpaper and redecorated the house from top to bottom.
* My daughters and I joined the local swimming club. They needed parents to help coach the children. So, I qualified as a swimming teacher to help there too.
* I also asked my neighbours to join me in a campaign to get trees planted along our street—which we achieved.

It sounds like a superwoman mask is something to aspire to—but it isn't. Wearing this mask—hiding my authentic self—nearly crippled me. Those around me saw my achievements and believed I was confident, energetic and on a mission to get things done. Yet the real me was exhausted, sad and lonely. I was running on empty. I was worried for my daughters after their dad had moved back to Japan. *How would they cope without him?* And despite knowing my husband and I were no longer two jigsaw pieces that perfectly fit together, I missed his presence in my life.

When I hit rock bottom, that evening when I sat at the bottom of the stairs with tears rolling down my cheeks, I knew I needed help. But I didn't know how to operate without what had become a familiar mask. Just the thought of showing up as the real me was scary. Yet over the next few years, as my healing journey unfolded, I discovered that life was easier without superwoman always in tow. I could still achieve a lot—I just needed to let others in and give myself much more self-love.

WHAT EXACTLY IS A MASK?

A mask is an adopted persona allowing us to show up in the world as a bigger, better or different version of who we are. Masks are worn for various reasons, but usually it is because we feel our authentic self is not good enough. For example, we may don the good daughter/son mask to meet our parents' expectations, even if it conflicts with our beliefs or desires. Or wear the diligent employee mask to prove we are worthy of a job promotion, even though we are filled with doubt. Or wear the loving partner mask to hide that we are upset by what our partner has said or done.

Do you recognise any of these common masks?

* The optimist mask paints a positive picture even when things don't look great.

* The I-can-do-this mask shows bravado and casts aside doubt.
* The creative genius mask allows us to be original, inventive and different.
* The work-persona mask gives us the confidence to perform our job as expected.
* The clown mask allows us to hide sadness while making others laugh.
* The I-am-in-charge mask provides us with the courage to lead others.

And so on, not forgetting the superman and superwoman masks which provide energy for herculean tasks.

THE COST OF THE CHARADE

Sometimes the adopted disguise simply gets us through a challenging moment—and it's not so different from who we are. Then, the energetic cost is minimal. However, when the gap between who we are and the character we pretend to be is vast, the energetic cost results in fatigue or even exhaustion.

Instinctively, we know that if we appear differently from how we presented ourselves in the past, there is a possibility of being rejected or hurt. Or we fear losing those we love. These are powerful reasons to cling to what we have created—even when our masked behaviour is making things worse rather than better.

Hiding our authentic selves stifles our unique viewpoints and creative ideas. If we choose to shine as we are, without hiding our imperfections, flaws or vulnerability, this paradoxically, makes us stronger. Being happy in our skin gives us more energy so we may reach our full potential. And if we shine our light, who knows what treasures may be found in the ripple effect of such changes.

HOW CLOTHING ENHANCES A MASK

Some uniforms are little more than a corporate branding exercise. Others visually indicate a specific job title which helps the wearer become that person too—like the pilot who not only looks the part but adopts the role when in uniform. The same is true for many others, such as soldiers, nurses and firefighters. When the first responders go to a road accident, they don't know whether the injuries people have sustained will be minor or horrific. Paramedics and police officers rely on their training for such incidents. And their uniform and work-persona mask keep them calm and professional even if they feel scared, horrified or out of their depth by what they are dealing with.

Even without a uniform, people often adopt a style of clothing to broadcast who they are. Intuitively, artists are more likely to choose colourful clothing, while most solicitors opt for a conservative business suit. Tradespeople often wear cargo trousers with multiple pockets for practicality, yet it also signals their work role. Chefs announce their status in the kitchen by the height of their white hat, and so it goes on.

REVEALING OUR TRUE SELVES

When someone has had a history of abuse, neglect or trauma, they are far more likely to wear a mask than those who have not suffered in this way. I'm not sure it is possible for anyone to live completely mask free, but, as with most things, it is about balance.

When our wonderful yet imperfect self is rarely shown to the world, we may feel like a fraud and lost because we too no longer know who we are. I see this in my friend, Hazel. She sees the world through a quirky lens and has such an infectious laugh. I love Hazel's ability to make everyone in her sphere laugh and smile. Hazel is a natural clown, yet she often wears it as a mask to stop prying eyes from seeing her sadness from the early deaths of her husband and both parents. When I met Sophie, a young client who came to The Jasmine House, she reminded me of Hazel.

SOPHIE'S STORY

Sophie greeted me on my doorstep with a broad smile and hugged me like a long-lost friend. By her feet was an assortment of travel bags and a case. It looked like she was moving in with me instead of staying for a three-day retreat. Sophie looked young—perhaps still in her twenties. Her long chestnut hair was worn loose, framing a pretty face with big brown eyes. She oozed a natural elegance, dressed simply in a figure-hugging black jersey dress and black ankle boots.

As I welcomed Sophie into my home, she gaily told me of the long tailback on the M3 due to an accident. Immediately, she continued that she had followed a tractor for miles through the New Forest, which she apologised, accounted for arriving late. Before I could sympathise about the traffic, Sophie laughingly added she had also missed a turn in Weymouth due to admiring the yachts in the harbour. As I led her upstairs to her room, her animated chattering continued, punctuated with gestures, flicks of her hair and broad smiles.

Later that afternoon, up in the Sky Room, I invited Sophie to sit in the armchair facing the view of Chesil Beach. Before I could ask how she was feeling and why she had come on this retreat, Sophie launched into her story. She had, she said, recently broken up with her boyfriend Rob and moved out of their shared flat. He had not been kind to her, she said, so overall it was good that this happened. She added she was now staying with Josie—her best friend. After six weeks of sleeping on her sofa, Sophie knew she had outstayed her welcome. Josie kept insisting it was OK, but Sophie knew that wasn't true.

I scribbled notes at a rate of knots as Sophie's story was told at lightning speed. She added how hard it was to find a suitable and affordable flat. And with a huge sigh, I heard that she didn't want to live somewhere that was pokey or dingy.

Like a gazelle being chased by a cheetah, Sophie suddenly changed direction. I heard how a rival company had bought out her boss's business and that she might face redundancy. Perhaps, she said, this wasn't a bad thing. Maybe a new start would be good for her. Then with another sigh, I heard her mum had been in hospital, so she hadn't yet told her about the break-up with Rob.

Finally, she paused and gave me a big smile as she said. 'It could be worse. I just need a little help from you to get me back on track.'

I took a moment. I had noticed how Sophie's story had been punctuated with incongruous smiles and half laughs. In that momentary silence, I felt Sophie's hidden sadness and saw how precarious she was in this situation. I sensed how much it was taking to hold it all together and how bravely she had put a positive spin on it all. Catching her eye, I said, 'Sophie, you are safe here. It's OK to be sad.'

For a moment, like a rabbit caught in the headlights of an oncoming car, Sophie was silent and still. Then tears began to slowly roll down her cheeks. I offered Sophie a tissue box and waited in gentle silence for her tears to subside.

'It's OK,' I reassured her. 'We can begin to sort this out.'

Over the next few days, Sophie and I looked at everything that had recently happened with Rob. Allowing herself to admit her true feelings—sadness, anger and fear—was a relief. Peeling away her overly optimistic mask gave permission to grieve the loss of Rob—a man she had thought was the one. She began to realise that pretending to be joyous all of the time may have contributed to Rob saying he didn't know who she was.

By nature, Sophie was bubbly and upbeat. This delightful part of her was not going to be erased by removing her mask—it merely allowed the other emotions to have a voice too.

HOW TO RECOGNISE YOUR MASKS

A tell-tale sign of using a mask detrimentally shows by being excessively concerned about what others think about you. Another sign is when a story of someone's suffering triggers feelings of sorrow, outrage or fear for this other person—yet you dismiss your hidden pain.

If only our masks were like fancy dress costumes we would recognise them, and taking them off would be easy. Having heavily invested in the pretence, it can be challenging to let go of the mask's protection.

THE CHALLENGES OF LETTING A MASK GO

Parents, teachers, culture, society and social media provide a narrow band of acceptable ways of being. When who we are on the inside—a self we consider to be less than perfect— doesn't meet the expectations of others, that's when we most often wear a mask. In these moments, our perception is that our true self won't be accepted, loved or respected. The idea of losing everything we treasure keeps a mask firmly in place.

Is there anything wrong with portraying a different self? Not always—but often, it's not beneficial to you or others when you constantly appear as someone else. How big is the gap between your true self and the one being portrayed? When the face you show to the world is far removed from the real you, at some point, the charade becomes too much to bear.

PEELING AWAY THE LAYERS OF YOUR MASKS

Are there areas of your life that you hide from the world? What if you could just be you—the good, the brilliant and the not-so-good parts of who you are? What would that feel like? Imagine for a moment showing up as your authentic self without fear, knowing it would be OK. Is this idea strong enough for you to peel away your mask—or at least some of it?

Before going further, bring to mind a close friend. Do you sometimes see them pretend to be someone or something they are not? As you recognise this, what does it arouse in you? Admiration for hiding their pain? Or anger that they are not being truthful or letting you in? Now flip the coin—what might they feel when they see you not being your authentic self?

STEPS TO REVEAL YOUR AUTHENTIC SELF

Relinquishing a mask that no longer serves you takes courage, but you can begin the process with these baby steps.

Begin by noticing situations where you use a mask to hide the real you. Be curious as to what triggers you to do this. Is it fear or something else? Give your mask a name. If you wish, make it a ridiculous or funny name—like superwoman—as this can help you spot it more easily. Consider the benefits of wearing this mask vs showing up as your true self. This first step is just to become more aware of what needs to change.

Now you are aware of how often this mask is worn, are you are ready to experiment with showing up as your genuine self? Try this out with people you trust and love. Summon the courage to share how you feel about something that matters—something you don't usually reveal. Witness what it feels like. Don't worry if it initially feels alien or you quickly chicken out. The more often you practise this, the easier it becomes.

When you are comfortable showing up as the real you with loved ones, it is time to widen the circle of people with whom you interact like this. Keep witnessing how it makes you feel and what changes in your interactions.

Finally, in time, showing up without your mask will feel more natural—like how you tie a shoelace or drive your car, and you will no longer need to consciously think about it. If you slip back into your old ways, simply look again at the triggers and the need to hide. Peeling away the layers of a mask brings you closer to a more effortless and happier life—something I wish for you to have.

Relinquish fear and anxiety

I learned that courage was not the absence of fear,
but the triumph over it.
The brave man is not he who does not feel afraid,
but he who conquers that fear.
♥ Nelson Mandela

Take a deep breath. How fearful or anxious do you feel in this moment? Is there a deep sense of calm in your body—or are your shoulders, neck and jaw tense? Is your mind clear and focused—or distracted by a hundred thoughts? Score out of ten how anxious you feel right now. A ten represents the maximum intensity of the feeling, while a one equals very little. Using this score, compare it to earlier today, yesterday, last week and a month ago. Are those scores higher or lower than now?

Contrasting the different anxiety levels provides perspective on how anxiety flows; you will see it isn't as constant as might be imagined. For example, perhaps yesterday everything went wrong and your anxiety levels were sky high, but today you feel better about what happened. Maybe last month life felt great, but a few days ago you received worrisome news which now whirs continually in your mind. Or perhaps last week you had to complete a new scary task, but having succeeded, you now have the confidence to repeat it. Every moment in everyday life constantly changes and evolves. Emotional responses match our life's dance, so even when anxiety feels constant, on closer inspection, it is rarely completely stuck.

THE INVISIBLE PANDEMIC OF ANXIETY

We're living in a world that's in a massive state of flux. The shifting sands under our feet are so palpable that it is causing chronic levels of worry and anxiety. Some say that the climate has changed before and that war, terror and life-threatening diseases are nothing new. Perhaps they are correct, but in earlier times, what happened beyond our shores was not widely known. The internet and digital technology daily bring news stories of war, famine, floods, disasters, wildfires, hunger and poverty into our lives. With witness accounts and upsetting imagery, watching these events or reading about them can make us feel helpless and disempowered. Taking on board all of this bad news can be overwhelming. And yet there is still a desire to know what is happening because our primal urge is to check whether or not we are safe.

The impact of our hectic lives, the widespread sense of insecurity, and the many who faced childhood trauma have contributed to huge number of people struggling with anxiety, stress and depression. These numbers aren't shown on our TV screens as the cases of Covid-19 were once tallied. So, the prevalence of anxiety in our societies is almost invisible. These recent statistics highlight the reality of the debilitating effects of chronic anxiety.

* Mind reports that in any given week in England 6 in 100 people will be diagnosed with generalised anxiety disorder.
* Mental Health UK has estimated that over 8 million people in the UK are experiencing an anxiety disorder at any one time.
* In March 2022, WHO stated that Covid-19 triggered a 25% increase in the prevalence of anxiety and depression worldwide.

We can't keep ignoring these numbers. Even if we feel anxiety free, we likely know someone who is suffering. People with severe anxiety may need professional help to regain their inner calm, but everyone can benefit from understanding how to lighten the impact of fear and anxiety that comes into our lives from all directions.

OVERVIEW OF THE FEAR EMOTIONS

FEAR
Uneasy
Cautious
Alarmed
Apprehensive
Nervous
Afraid
Fearful
Worried
Anxious
Jumpy
Frightened
Scared
Panicky
Terrified
Petrified

At times, we have all been afraid, frightened, scared or even terrified. We know there are degrees of fear—like those listed here—yet we rarely understand how the fear response functions. Even less well-known is the importance of releasing fear's energy after a scary event has passed.

The purpose of fear is to keep us safe. In essence, when a threat or danger is sensed, fear ignites the body's energy system. It also provides resources so we can deal with whatever we are facing. And then, our intuition guides us on the actions we need to take to stay safe.

After a threat has dissolved or danger has passed, some fear energy usually remains in the body—which needs to be released. Talking about what happened, shimmying, shaking, dancing and sometimes crying all help the body do this. If though the cycle of fear is not fully completed, it becomes restless energy, often resulting in feelings of anxiety.

EXPLORING ANXIETY

Anxiety typically arises from multiple worries and concerns that have snowballed. Anxiety can begin with anything—demands from our family, stress at work, financial uncertainty, or health concerns. Often several issues amalgamate, rolling around in the pit of the stomach. Trying to calm a multitude of concerns in different areas of our life can quickly become overwhelming.

Anxiety heightens with a sense of unease about something that is happening or might happen in the future. This is a natural response to sensing danger for ourselves, those we love, as well as scary events that threaten us from afar. After the danger has passed, then all fearful emotions are meant to dissipate. However, anxiety may remain in the psyche, triggering endless eddies of concern and worry. When our fear responses are out of balance in this way, our intuition is also stifled. Without free-flowing intuition, we are more easily startled by unexpected loud noises or sudden movements because we are less able to judge what is safe and what isn't.

Panic or terror can arise within us in less than a nanosecond. However, most fearful emotions begin with a sense of apprehension, and this unease sets off our alarm bells, activating a host of mind and body reactions. We become hyper-alert which enables us to see, hear, feel, smell and sense things more acutely than usual. The additional information gained from our super-charged senses allows the subconscious to rapidly activate reactions. Our intuition guides us to move or freeze, shout or stay silent. How strongly we react is dependent on the perceived threat to our survival.

To deal with the threat—whether it's real or perceived—the body ramps up our energy. Blood sugar and adrenaline levels rise, and the digestive system receives less blood so more can flow into the limbs. This happens because digesting our last meal is considered less important than surviving. Temporarily, more energy is also given to the part of the brain that instantaneously reacts. Now our body is primed and ready.

These natural fear responses—fight, flight or freeze—evolved during our ancient history. Back then, fear was more often triggered when facing a wild animal, a marauding tribe or a hostile clan member. In the aftermath, when all was calm, our ancient ancestors probably did what other mammals do—trembled, perhaps danced or shook to release pent-up energy. Whether they did this and we have forgotten, we will never know. But there is another reason why we might not naturally do this. Our lives today are more complex, hectic and frenetic than theirs were. Their chances of facing dangerous wild animals were relatively high—for us, it would be incredibly rare. And yet our body still responses as if we need to run away or get ready to fight.

An example of how shaking off fear happens in the animal world can be found on YouTube. Search for 'Impala shaking off trauma'. The video begins with a leopard pinning an impala to the ground. Before the leopard delivers a death bite to the impala's throat, it is distracted by a hyena and a troop of baboons. Spooked, the leopard releases its hold and slinks away, leaving the impala unharmed. Still immobile from the shock, the impala begins to breathe deeply, inflating its belly like a balloon. Then the impala attempts to get up, but it stumbles, legs wobbly and its body shaking violently. After a couple of minutes, the shaking stops, the fear energy has been released, and the impala trots off to join the herd.

MY STORY: TREMBLING ON THE ROADSIDE

On my first day back in the office after a holiday, when I had a graphic design business, I was surprised to find an appointment booked in my diary to see Chris. In the past, Chris had been a regular customer—we had produced his quarterly newsletters, product sheets and other printed materials. During that time, I regularly visited Chris at his offices to discuss these printing projects, but our last meeting, six months earlier, had not gone well. After the usual pleasantries, Chris waved two quotes from other companies in front of me. They were offering to do the newsletters and product sheets, for a lot less money.

Long story short, Chris asked me to match their prices, and I said no. Chris was stunned by my instant response. He was a charming man but not easy to work with. Regularly, three-quarters of the way through any project he would have a new idea. This would entail new photos and/or different text—the latter invariably would not fit the allocated space. My team and I had become accustomed to the higher levels of work to complete his projects, and, in part, this was taken into account with my prices. Even so, our profit margins were still slim.

As that meeting had come to a close, I was still churned up. I felt ambushed but managed a smile and thanked Chris for his custom. As I left, I said he could call me if he changed his mind. Not that I believed he would. The other company's prices were significantly lower than mine.

So, on the allotted day of this new meeting, I drove to the Oxford Science Park, wondering why Chris wanted to see me. Perhaps, I thought, there was a mistake on one of his technical product sheets that we had designed and printed. I couldn't imagine why else he wanted to see me.

In the reception area, I signed the visitor book, and waited for Chris's PA to collect me. But it wasn't his PA who arrived. Instead, it was Chris— something he never did. As we walked to his office, he was his most charming self, politely enquiring about my holiday and family. He guided me through his office suite and straight into the meeting room. Spread across the boardroom table were copies of our newsletters and product sheets. Fanned out beside them were those produced by the new company. The contrast was stark. I instantly saw that the newer work had colour and branding inconsistencies, and the paper looked cheap. I also noticed their newsletters had blocks of text in a font size that was almost too small to read. I assumed this was how they coped with Chris providing too much text.

Sheepishly, Chris pointed to the work designed by the other company.

'These don't look great, do they?'

'No,' I agreed.

Chris's demeanour softened. 'Jennie, I know our last meeting didn't go well, but I'm hoping you will agree to work with me again.'

I smiled, 'Yes—but it will be at our old rates.'

He smiled back, 'Of course.'

With this resolved, we sat down to discuss his new project.

Driving back to my office, I mulled over new ideas for Chris. I was vaguely aware that the A34 dual carriageway was busy but no more than usual. As I approached an articulated lorry in the slow lane, I indicated to overtake. I was almost parallel with the lorry's tail lights when its indicator lights flashed on. I assumed the driver would wait until I had passed, but the lorry immediately started to move into the fast lane.

In that second, I registered I'd seen continental speed stickers on the back of the trailer and realised it was a left-hand drive vehicle. I must be in his blind spot, I thought. I braked but not hard because another car was close behind me. The lorry then braked and headed back towards the slow lane. The rapid change of direction caused the trailer to snake towards my car. The gap of clear road in front of me was narrowing fast. Without thinking, I floored the accelerator. My car wheels thumped loudly over the white ribbed safety line, leaving me inches from the metal barrier on my right. I sped past the lorry in seconds, and then manoeuvred back into the fast lane.

I checked my rear-view mirror and saw that the lorry driver had regained control and the car behind me must have dropped back. I suddenly felt nauseous. Ahead was the big lay-by just before the M40 junction. Accelerating once more, I crossed the slow lane and slid into a wide gap between two parked lorries. Opening my car door, I stumbled out and managed to get to the grass verge before I threw up. Alarmingly, my body then began to shake. For a moment, I thought it was an earthquake, like the one I had experienced in Jakarta. I held on to my car to steady myself. *What is happening to me?* My entire body shook for what seemed ages, but it was probably only a minute or two. Then, as suddenly as it had started, the shaking stopped. Reaching into my jacket pocket, I found a crumpled tissue and dabbed my lips dry. Still not trusting my legs, I used the car as a crutch to walk around to the driver's door. Sitting inside, I felt the car shaking. Panic rose once more until I realised it was just the vibration from the traffic zipping past the lay-by.

I sat for another ten minutes before trusting myself to drive. I set off and drove slowly to the office. Once there, I shared what had happened with my team. It had been a lucky escape, I said. Then I began sharing my design ideas for Chris's new project.

CAUSES OF ANXIETY

How anxious people feel about events, situations or daily life varies tremendously. What is scary for one person is a piece of cake for another. However, some harrowing life events often lead to underlying and prolonged anxiety. The most common of these are:

* Childhood abuse, abandonment or neglect.
* Experiencing armed conflict—either as military personnel or surviving such events.
* Accidents that caused severe injuries to you and or loved ones.
* Witnessing close-up, tragic events or disasters.
* Being diagnosed with a serious illness.
* A history of depression and mental health difficulties.

SYMPTOMS OF CHRONIC ANXIETY

It is easy to become accustomed to living with low-level anxiety. So much so that we may not recognise the impact on our behaviour or how our body responds. Do you regularly struggle with the following symptoms?

HOW THE BODY RESPONDS	EMOTIONAL RESPONSES	BEHAVIOURAL CHANGES
Headache, neck or back pain	Constantly on edge	Avoiding anything fearful
Digestive issues	Sense of dread	Escapism
Brain fog	Catastrophising	Abusing alcohol or drugs
Heart palpitations	Irritable	Comfort eating
Difficulty in sleeping	Restless	Isolation
Sweating or clammy hands	Bored	Reckless risk-taking

These symptoms, shown in the table above, might be caused by other things. But, if you sense they are connected to anxiety, ask yourself—how long have these been part of your life? Anchor your memories by using life's milestones. Did you, for example, have these symptoms on your last birthday? What about the birthday before that? Identifying the time these symptoms occurred may highlight what originally triggered your fears. Be curious about different possibilities—there may be more than one cause.

EXPERIENCING FREE-FLOWING FEAR

In isolated areas of South America, Africa and Asia, indigenous people live life in ways not so different from our ancient ancestors. And virtually all of them have a tradition of storytelling. Some are fables, yet most are current experiences, especially tales about overcoming fearful encounters with large cats, poisonous snakes and other wild animals. Their scary moments and successes provide rich and powerful lessons about fear. Storytelling is, and always has been, a big part of our lives. And we all love scary stories with happy endings.

To experience free-flowing fear, try this visualisation along similar lines. Imagine yourself in a remote, rural area of India. You are standing in an open, grassy area close to the edge of a jungle. Suddenly you feel uneasy. Scanning the scrub, bushes and grass, you suddenly sense movement. As your eyes hone in on the spot, you are stunned to see a tiger camouflaged by a patch of longer grass. Its hazel eyes are staring at you. Transfixed, the hairs on your neck prickle, and your heart begins to race. The pungent, musky smell of the tiger hits your nostrils. Petrified, your breathing becomes shallow. You notice a thick branch lying on the ground—its leaves are green, so it's not rotted yet. Peripheral vision allows you to estimate that the small shack, with its door slightly ajar, is about ten metres away. In the momentary stillness, your subconscious weighs up running to the shack, using the branch or staying completely still. The tiger sniffs the air, turns, and pads back into the jungle.

Did you get a sense of the tension that fear brings? And a realisation that after the danger had passed you would need to release this pent-up energy?

DISSOCIATING FROM FEAR

For children growing up in an abusive or violent home, the face of the scary tiger might also be the face of someone they love. The line between what is safe and what isn't becomes fuzzy. To cope, children may dissociate from the fear—as I did with my granddad. For those of us who are like the swans, dissociation may also become a habit in adulthood.

Its once protective energy in childhood now may take the lessons of fear away from us. This happens because dissociation sweeps away the painful experiences and life's lessons. Without earlier memories or red flags to guide us, we may repeatedly make the same mistakes. Poor behaviour from others directed towards us intuitively feels wrong, but we may not be able to recall what was the best course of action from last time. The uneasiness of these situations often ends up as unidentified anxiety.

One way to heal this form of anxiety is to write in a journal daily, especially on days when things are challenging. Focusing on your feelings and observations makes it less likely that they will be swept from memory.

FEARLESSNESS AND RECKLESSNESS

When fear is buried so deep inside, it's no longer available to keep you safe. Fearless people often declare life is for living and claim others are scaredy-cats. These declarations are often made just before embarking on something foolhardy or dangerous.

Car racers, stunt performers, elite military personnel and endurance athletes may seem fearless in their work, but usually they are not. Rather, the vast majority take the utmost care to stay safe while performing their risky feats. By contrast, someone with no fear takes enormous risks with their safety and sometimes that of others.

Often this fearlessness is driven by the need to feel an adrenaline rush to provide a high. Escaping a close shave can lead to a euphoric sense of being alive and it can be addictive. Such fearlessness may also indicate that the person is trying to force open the limiting effects that anxiety imposes on life.

DEEP BREATHING TO RELINQUISH ANXIETY

Thích Nhất Hạnh was a Vietnamese Buddhist and a renowned spiritual leader and peace activist. On the next page is one of his quotations which reminds us how we can use breathing to lessen the grip of anxiety:

Breath is the bridge which connects life to consciousness, which unites your body to your thoughts. Whenever your mind becomes scattered, use your breath as the means to take hold of your mind again.

When we are fearful and readying ourselves to react, our breathing becomes shallow. And if the fear energy is not entirely dissipated, breathing lightly may become our norm. It's like the body is hovering over the accelerator, ready at any moment to return to survival mode. When we breathe shallowly, it tells the body, *I don't feel safe.*

Slow, rhythmic, conscious breathing, by contrast, has a remarkable effect on the body. It calms the mind, body and nervous system, switches off the fear responses and, in effect, spreads the message *I am safe.* Surprisingly, these changes happen quickly. With just ten deep breaths, you can easily bring a sense of inner calm to the mind, body and nervous system.

Try this breathing exercise. Choose somewhere quiet and either lie down or sit comfortably. Now breathe in through your nose. Keep your shoulders still and imagine the air is filling a balloon in your belly. When you feel full of air, hold your breath for a second. Now exhale through your mouth, using your diaphragm and ribs to squeeze the air out of your lungs. It helps to make a haaa sound as you exhale. Repeat ten times. Notice that breathing like this is like a mini workout, yet the effort should not be strained or forced. After these ten breaths, allow your breathing to return to normal.

Take a second to notice how you are feeling. Do you feel calmer? Are you able to see things slightly differently than a few minutes ago?

To practise another breathing exercise that also helps with this, on YouTube, search for 'Wim Hof Guided Breathing'.

SHAKING TO RELEASE PENT-UP FEAR

Several therapies actively involve shaking to release anxiety and trauma from the body's nervous system. Somatic Experiencing includes shaking too, and I found it to be helpful for me. Somatic Experiencing was created by Peter Levine. His book, *Waking The Tiger*, explains how trauma—big and small—can become trapped in the body.

Below is my way of shaking which combines several different techniques that I have learnt. Begin by considering what feelings you would like to release. Is it something that happened today—or something you sense needs completion from your past? Without going into detail, simply set your intention to let this fear or anxiety flow from your body.

Find a safe place to move around. Remove your shoes and socks. Now begin by shaking your arms and hands actively but not violently. After about fifteen seconds of shaking, rest your arms. Then lift one leg off the floor and shake it. If you need to hold on to something for balance, that's OK. After around fifteen seconds, switch legs. Now plant both feet firmly on the ground. Shake and wriggle your body somewhat more than if you were dancing on the spot. Do this also for around fifteen seconds. These stated times when read seem short, but when you do it, fifteen seconds feels like a long time. Repeat the sequence.

Shaking in this way may be easy or challenging for you—it's OK if you need to stop and catch your breath. After the second round of shaking, stamp your feet for a count of ten. Then, loosely swing your arms and twist your torso to the left and right. Finally, take in three deep breaths. How do you feel now? What do you sense has shifted in your feelings for the set intention? It may only be a subtle change for the better—but that's good. Often it takes several rounds of shaking to let go of old emotional energy. Try this exercise every day for a week—when you first wake up is a good time. Shaking will help you reset your nervous system and discharge remnants of past fears.

ONE MORE TIP

If at any time you experience a scary incident, in the aftermath don't quash the fear with the words *I am OK*. It's natural to want to brush the fear away, but if you can, allow time to release the excess energy. Do this by moving, not just standing or sitting, and if you can, consciously shake. When you feel calmer, re-run the event through your mind and tell someone what happened to you. These simple steps complete the fear cycle and release any remnant of its energy from your body.

You are good enough— just as you are

Perfectionism is not a quest for the best.
It is a pursuit of the worst in ourselves,
the part that tells us that nothing we do
will ever be good enough—that we should try again.
♥ Julia Cameron

Do you believe you are good enough—just as you are? Or are there niggling doubts? Would saying or even thinking *I am good enough* feel cringeworthy, boastful or egotistical?

By nature, most of us are not comfortable announcing to the world our good-enoughness, but let's flip this idea. Would the opposite viewpoint, believing we are not worthy, feel more acceptable? Probably not. So, that leaves an interesting dilemma. Which parts of you are good enough—and which aren't?

Feeling inferior to others may start out as being naturally timid or the result of something that happened. More usually, it is a collection of experiences that led to feelings of doubt. Below are some typical reasons why people feel less worthy than others.

* It may be down to innate shyness that leads to perceiving others as better.
* Unhealed, past trauma often leaves people feeling less. It is not

always easy to put your finger on precisely what this is, yet it hovers in the background of life.

* Children who are neglected, abused or harmed often believe they have done something wrong which has led to an adult mistreating them. A young child rarely considers that the adult is at fault.

* Self-esteem begins with love and care given by parents. However, if one or both parents still carry unhealed emotional scars, they don't feel worthy either. Unwittingly, they may pass on feelings of unworthiness to their children.

* Parents, teachers and family members may unfavourably compare one offspring against another. Sometimes, the intention is to provide motivation, but this often fails.

* And sadly, some of you reading this were bluntly told you were a hopeless case, useless and unimportant. The extrapolation leads to thoughts that you are unlovable and unworthy.

Be curious about any person's opinion of how worthy you are—even if that is a parent's view. Determine whether their words were driven by their unhealed wounds, uncontrolled anger or an agenda which had nothing to do with you.

Feeling not good enough is widespread, yet we don't fully see it as so many people mask these emotions. Suffering from low self-esteem, people will subconsciously seek approval in the eyes of others—often going to extraordinary lengths to attain this. They believe succeeding in impressing someone else will make them feel OK. And so, they work long hours without asking for overtime. Or they attempt to be the perfect mum, dad, son, daughter, friend or partner. Often low self-esteem leads to fulfilling the needs of partners and friends above their own. Walking along such a path is exhausting, as it's virtually impossible to be at peace with yourself.

This tactic of seeking recognition through the eyes of others rarely improves self-esteem. Being dependent on their opinions is like walking over quicksand. At any moment, this person may change their mind or move away, or they may not reaffirm the sought-after worthiness. Self-esteem has to come from our heart and mind. Being content with who we are means being comfortable in our own skin. It's about accepting that we are not perfect. We all have flaws, quirks and foibles—and we are still OK.

To change how you see your self-worth, begin with the idea that every day brings a new opportunity to learn more, be a better version of yourself, and shine even more brightly. We all have something special to contribute to life. It doesn't have to be grandiose.

Sarah, who lives in my village, contributes in this way. She is semi-retired and loves gardening. When she spots an unloved garden in the village, she asks the owner if, as a project, she can work there for free. I'm sure no one refuses. With this new project, she gives an hour or so a week, as and when she can fit it in. Slowly, she begins to transform their garden. She encourages the house owner to engage with their garden too and makes it easy to maintain. Over the space of a year, the garden becomes lovely once more. Sarah shines in this way. I have witnessed her work personally—one of my neighbours no longer has a garden full of brambles!

We are all on our journeys through life. Some people are ahead of us, some are behind, and some are roughly in the same place on their path. Today, you are in the perfect place for you. And when the sun comes up tomorrow, there will be another opportunity for you to become the person you wish to be.

YOU ARE ATTRACTIVE

Watching a recent documentary on the Egyptian Pharaohs, it seems even back then we were programmed to care about how we look. Beauty perhaps did and still does wield influence. But today, it feels like there is an obsession to look younger, slimmer, smell divine and wear the latest fashions.

Marketeers and social media have played a major role in this. Scrolling through feeds on our mobiles, it is rare to find unflattering photos of friends, and everyone in ad-world looks beautiful. Social media is not interested in the ordinary, mundane or the times when we don't look picture-perfect.

Looking different from the narrow band of what is deemed beautiful can dent our self-esteem. All, though, is not what it seems in the world of beautiful people. Try this. Google 'Celebrity before and after Photoshop'. See how staggeringly different the *after* photos look. Spotty complexions, unflattering curves, wrinkles and crooked teeth have been digitally enhanced to perfection. Sometimes, even necks have been elongated and eyebrows literally raised to give the appearance of youth. So, photos of the famous—those we see on social media, in magazines, ads and, even on occasion in the movies—may look natural but most often they aren't.

The above helps us remember these much-loved people are more like us than we thought. And, like us, they don't look brilliant first thing in the morning. True, some celebrities have won the beauty-gene jackpot, but no one can prevent wrinkles and certain body parts from drifting south with age. Please take a fresh look at what you don't like about yourself. You are OK. Most likely far more than OK—attractive in a way that is unique to you. And if you are not convinced, choose to work on enhancing nature's gift to you without beating yourself up or spending a fortune.

Even if you believe there are justifiable reasons for feeling less attractive than others, know that you and everyone are far more than looks alone. You are a precious soul, and true beauty shines from within. Some of the most attractive people on the planet are *not* blessed with traditional beauty. They have accepted who they are and how they look. It's their inner confidence that makes them shine.

Take a moment to consider who isn't conventionally pretty or handsome yet is still attractive. What is it that appeals to you? Can you modify an element of what they have—how they dress, walk or talk—and turn it into your own style?

THE GIFT OF YOUR UNIQUENESS

Among the billions of people living on our planet, you are unique. No one has walked in your shoes and shared the same highs and lows, events, adventures, traumas, lessons and illnesses. Even identical twins with the same DNA have different gut biology, thoughts, beliefs and values. No one is *exactly* like you.

Accepting and honouring your uniqueness helps stop the need to compare yourself with others. Friends, peers or those you perceive have attained more than you have haven't lived your life. If they had, who knows what their life would look like now. We rarely know the whole story about how people reached where they are—or why they haven't. Begin by letting go of seeing them as better. Instead, see they are simply different from you.

IMPERFECTLY PERFECT

Imagine for a moment that you made friends with someone perfectly perfect. At work, at home, in life and even in friendship they are flawless. For a while, having such a friend would be great. What would happen, though, on a disastrous day at work? Would your perfect friend understand how awful you feel or that you needed to rant to release the pressure? Probably not. A flawless friend may be unable to empathise because their worldview would not contain similar experiences.

Our best friends aren't perfect, but they typically will be there for us when we have had a bad day. So, now we have to ask ourselves—what drives our desire to be perfect when it would not be desirable in a friend? Can you accept yourself as imperfectly perfect?

LETTING GO OF IMPOSTOR SYNDROME

Successful people are not immune to questioning their self-worth. The pressure to be constantly successful is massive at certain points in a career.

Impostor syndrome manifests itself with the belief that success has been achieved through a series of lucky breaks rather than hard work. Fearing people will see through the subterfuge, these people work harder than ever and usually micro-manage to stay in control. They take perfectionism to the nth degree and expect it from their colleagues and team too. Even with all this extra effort, they rarely feel satisfied and can't relax, because, in their eyes, they haven't done enough.

Imposter syndrome can also show up in people who have beaten the odds. For example, when people have lost a massive amount of weight, or achieved a first-class honours degree through home study, or completed an arduous challenge. Despite being worthy of their achievements, they feel it was down to other factors and feel uncomfortable when they receive praise for their accomplishments.

When identifying with the imposter syndrome, gently ask how it serves you. What would it be like to trust that you have done enough? Also, no matter how hard we work, there will always be more to do tomorrow. We have limits. So, without egotism, acknowledge what you have achieved. Even with some luck, success still requires determination, hard work, plus the ability to get back up when others give up.

WHO IS JUDGING YOU?

Consider, for a moment, who judges you as not good enough? Did someone tell you or imply it? Such words from a parent are soul-destroying and often resonate for decades after they were spoken. We all want our parents to be proud of who we are and what we have achieved. Looking into the shadows, what if they were unable to encourage you due to their pain, insecurities or fears? Through the eyes of an adult, and now perhaps a parent yourself, can you forgive them for what they did or said? Their words were an opinion which was not necessarily a true reflection of you or the situation.

Anytime we are harshly criticised, it is challenging. A one-off comment might be unfair, but it can be brushed aside. Occasionally, the words said are a consequence of our mistakes, but being constantly mocked or derided is not OK. If someone is always picking fault with you, are they perhaps threatened by your presence, achievements or potential? Are they snubbing your achievements to protect themselves? If this rings true, pop back to the chapter, *Restoring Your Boundaries* and check whether you need to reinstate them with this person.

We tend to judge ourselves far more harshly than anyone else would. In this case, come back to the idea that you are OK. When a mistake is made, own it, then do what you can to make amends. Then actively choose to let go of being hard on yourself.

CHANGE YOUR INNER DIALOGUE

Doubts about self-esteem may be made worse when our inner critic goes into overdrive. We all have multiple inner voices which provide us with guidance. As well as the critic's voice, other key ones include; the caretaker, responsible adult, inner child, intuition and rebel. Sometimes one inner voice becomes dominant, drowning the other voices and skewing the picture of what is happening.

To quieten the inner critic voice, internally thank it for its presence and also notice how often you berate yourself. Would a friend be so critical about what happened? No. A good friend would take in the bigger picture, remind you of what else is happening and offer empathy.

It's surprising how many people don't wish to be kind to themselves. They see it as being let off the hook. But if we have a situation that needs resolving, and then we pile self-criticism on top of this, it makes resolving the issue far more challenging. A kindly voice acknowledges the problem and offers encouragement to try again.

TODAY–BE THE BEST YOU CAN BE

Marianne Williamson wrote a beautiful poem used in Nelson Mandela's inaugural speech. It begins with:

> *Our deepest fear is not that we are inadequate.*
> *Our deepest fear is that we are powerful beyond measure.*
> *It is our light, not our darkness that most frightens us.*
> *We ask ourselves, 'Who am I to be brilliant, gorgeous,*
> *talented, fabulous?*

Our fear of not being good enough is a double-edged sword. Deep inside, a part of us believes we are good enough—or mostly so. But the idea of shining, standing up for our beliefs and perhaps being different from others can be scary.

Is hiding your light connected to a fear of losing friends, money, job or status within your family? Is it safer to hide away than speak up, join a group, apply for a promotion, go on a date, or even tell a friend some home truths? Imagine for a minute doing something you previously felt you couldn't do. What is the worst that could happen? There may be some embarrassment, or someone might say no. Yet very often, standing up and shining outweighs any shadowy fears. Oliver Wendell Holmes once said, *Many people die with their music still in them*. Please don't be one of the many. Be brave, shine, dance, sing, play and be your glorious self.

BOOSTING YOUR SELF-ESTEEM

Changing how we see ourselves and the resulting new behaviour begins with a choice; in this instance, choosing to see your own worthiness. Choice alone doesn't make it happen—yet it is where it begins.

Reflect on your wonderful uniqueness. One way of doing this is to consider five ways you are different from others. Perhaps you have unusual physical characteristics, have had big adventures in life, or have a hidden talent. No one will create a list that is exactly the same as yours. Without giving it much thought, here is my list.

* I have lived and worked in France.
* My ex-husband is Japanese.
* I am a strong sea swimmer.
* Dentists tell me I have an unusual bite as my front teeth can't touch.
* I sold our home and bought a smaller one to afford a much-promised, round-the-world trip with my daughters.

Supposing instead I had worked in Germany, married a British guy, had a perfect bite, and had taken my daughters on another, once-in-a-lifetime adventure. All of that would be OK, maybe even better than my life, but I would not be the same person I am today. Try creating another list of five. You could do this endlessly, but I'm sure you get it. There is no one exactly like you, and that's great. Be you!

Learn how to celebrate your successes. I'm not suggesting you throw parties. Instead, it helps to regularly acknowledge what you have achieved in life. We are programmed to keep looking for the next thing on an endless to-do list, which makes us think we haven't completed anything. Take a moment to admire a completed project, a room you have tidied, or a delicious meal you have prepared. Doing this regularly changes your perception of who you are and what you can achieve.

Enjoy too the successes of family and friends. Celebrate and be happy for them, and remember their journey is not better, just different from yours. Admire what they have achieved. It's OK to be curious about how they succeeded and see what can be learnt, but don't try to be them. Being you is special enough.

Lastly, can you take elements from a successful area of your life and apply them to a situation that is not currently rosy? There are always new ways of doing something or being someone. Choose to be the person that deep down you know you want to be. What will be your first step as a person with high self-esteem?

Healing a broken heart

It's hard to turn the page,
When you know someone won't be in the next chapter.
But, the story must go on.
♥ Thomas Wilder

Are you at peace with your relationships that didn't work out? Think back to earlier boyfriends, girlfriends, partners or spouses. Is your heart clear of sadness, anger or jealousy? If yes—YAY!—then there is no need to read this chapter. But if your history with ex-partners hasn't been great, or there's a pattern of relationship disasters, or your heart is right now aching, please read on.

WHY DOES A BREAK-UP HURT SO MUCH?

In the days after a break-up, the wretchedness of a broken heart hurts like hell. We feel sad, lost, angry and sometimes afraid. Jealousy, shame and regret may be in the mix too. The emotional onslaught typically takes away the appetite and makes for sleepless nights. In the early days after a break-up, tears may flow after the tiniest of triggers, leaving a pile of soggy tissues in their wake.

At night, alone in bed and unable to sleep, the mind spins endlessly—*Why did they leave me? What did I do wrong? What happened to us?* During the day, there is little peace as the head re-runs conversations and arguments, looking for clues to answer the many questions of why. And it is impossible to focus on anything for long.

Once upon a time, things between you and your partner were very different. Months, years or decades ago—when you first exchanged the words *I love you*—a magical spell was cast. In that moment of being seen, heard, accepted and loved, you landed on cloud nine. Floating high above everyday niggles, you hoped that life would be forever this wonderful.

In the early, heady days of being newly in love, life is as near perfect as it can be. Yet we can't stop the flow of life and the difficulties of everyday stuff happening with family, work, money, and home. To successfully deal with this stuff, a couple has to navigate differences in upbringing, values, needs and personality traits. Most difficulties in a relationship can be resolved with love, good communication and kindness. No one lives in a perfect world—bumps in the road appear for everyone.

When two people first become a couple, their souls create a unique melody for their dance through life. Sometimes it's like a loving waltz, occasionally it's a dramatic tango, and frequently it's like a quickstep to cope with the hectic pace of life. In the mix there maybe the seduction of a salsa and perhaps times of mum-and-dad dancing around the kitchen. The many steps taken over weeks, months and years forge a strong bond, enabling a couple to deal with the odd missteps. As the relationship matures, the words *I love you* act as reassurance that the bond is still strong.

Some dances last a lifetime. Some only for a short while. No one can guarantee how long the music will play or whether one day it will miss a beat. Most dances are worthy of the effort to get back into step. Yet if both are out of sync for a long time, and it feels impossible, one partner will end the dance with the words *It's over*. All of those precious steps taken together now appear to count for nothing.

The pain of a broken heart lies in the gap between *I love you* and *It's over*.

GENTLE GRIEVING

I wish I had a magic wand to take away the pain of a broken heart, but like grieving, which in part it is, it takes time to heal. Regardless of the relationship's ending, grieving the loss of what could have been but wasn't— is still necessary.

The length of grieving depends on how long you were together, whether you have children, need to divorce or had joint investments, as well as your personality types. The more entwined your lives were, the longer sorting out practicalities takes, which often delays the healing process.

Listening to your heart and soul will help you gauge how long you need to grieve. Typically, it is somewhere between three months to slightly more than a year. One day, you will find yourself humming a favourite tune or laughing at something silly on the TV. Catch your smile in that moment— even if it is fleeting. This is a sign that things are changing for the better. From this day on, your pain will be noticeably less than the day before. And the day after, lighter still, until one day you will wake up feeling OK.

Time is a great healer, but you don't have to simply wait it out—there are things you can do to hasten your healing.

Heartache is at its worst when the emotions aren't flowing but just cycling. To get back into flow, emotions need an outlet.

Crying it all out releases sadness. People fear if they begin to cry, they will never stop. Yet tears cannot flow indefinitely. Sobbing, when allowed to continue for as long as needed, naturally ceases. And that happens in far less time than you may imagine.

Talking things through with someone you trust definitely helps emotions flow again. Shame, in particular, dissipates when the story is sacredly shared. Journaling provides space to record rational commentary along with emotional outpouring.

Anger is a natural cleansing emotion that can help you restore boundaries. If you feel you have been trampled on, revisit the chapter,

Restore Your Boundaries, to remind yourself how to re-establish yours.

Conscious Writing, sometimes known as Direct Writing, is helpful too. For this exercise, take a few sheets of paper and write whatever pops into your mind. It is not important to check spelling or punctuation. Simply keep writing until you have several pages of notes. Some of it won't make much sense when you read it back, which is totally OK. However, some words and phrases will leap off the page. These words are the real reason for the exercise, as they often reveal insights about your true feelings about what is happening.

During your grieving, be gentle with yourself. Trust your instincts to figure out what works best for you and when to implement these healing steps. Allow time to honour what worked well in your relationship because there were happy and good times earlier in your dance. Doing this helps restore balance to your story.

Your book of life contains many chapters. The latest one about you and your ex-partner is closing. Some lessons learnt on your journey with your ex-partner will be carried forward. Others, those not entirely completed, may need to be revisited. Every new chapter opens possibilities for being happier and emotionally healthier in life. Your next chapter could be the best one yet.

UNDERSTANDING INITIAL ATTRACTION

When you first met your ex-partner, there was a magnetic attraction. Pheromones, personality, preferences and future possibilities were all part of that pull. Yet if earlier emotional pain still resides in the psyche, another part of the attraction will have come from the subconscious. Wounded souls—the swans—instantly recognise one another as fellow survivors. Being seen in this way is very seductive. And if two wounded souls come together, their dance will inevitably include some of their past histories. Old behaviour, dressed differently but in essence the same, frequently repeats itself.

Subconsciously, the attraction of two such souls can be healing. Old ways have to be seen and consciously worked on together. Then such a relationship can blossom into something incredibly rare and special. Sadly, many such relationships still repeat old histories and keep the pain alive. If you recognise this as part of your pattern, in the future, look for signs of this before starting a new relationship that ultimately won't be healthy.

When we are attracted to a potential partner, we are curious. *Who is this person—deep in their soul? What matters to them, and what are their dreams?* We score and compare their answers to our needs on an internal tick chart in our heads. As the relationship grows stronger, we consider if our dreams can be entwined with theirs.

However, our checklists are somewhat flawed. During the first few months of dating, we are not our true selves—and neither are they. Rather, we present our best selves to one another. To see this, recall early magical dates. When getting ready to meet your love interest, did you take more time and care than usual with your appearance? While on the date, did you share stories that showed you in a favourable light or made them laugh? Probably. We want our love interest to find us attractive, so we put on a good show because we don't wish to scare the person away. We carefully hide parts of ourselves that may be off-putting and are more tolerant when things don't go to plan. We may even express an interest in a topic they like that we have previously declared to be boring! Our best self does all of this to keep the other person interested.

It sounds manipulative, but deep down, it's not a lie. We are sometimes kind, caring, thoughtful and generous, and at others, unkind, selfish and thoughtless. This is our light and shadow at play. Our best self is our light—the person we want to be and sometimes are. Excluding all of our shadow requires a massive amount of conscious effort.

Why can't we always be our best selves? Being our best self requires conscious effort, which is puny compared to the powerhouse of the subconscious. The statistics are staggering. Scientists have proven that the subconscious can process around twenty million environmental stimuli per second compared to just forty by the conscious mind. Scientists also state that eighty per cent of our life is run subconsciously. That's a scary thought!

We get a glimpse of how this works by considering how we drive. In the driver's seat, do you consciously think *mirror, signal, manoeuvre* before turning or overtaking? Or does this sequence of actions happen naturally? As experienced drivers, our subconscious does most of the work for us. It scans traffic movements and street signs while at the same time being aware of pedestrians, cats and anything out of the ordinary. Without a second thought, we accelerate, brake and change gears. As our subconscious driving does most of the work for us, we can sing along to songs or plan the day ahead. This is very different from when we first learnt to drive. Without the subconscious's assistance—it was not yet programmed—you had to do everything consciously, which was exhausting.

Being our best self at all times requires masses of conscious effort. When we feel comfortable with someone, as we relax, more of our subconscious programs take over. As our true self pops up, with our fingers crossed we hope our potential partner likes our authentic self. And, of course, they hope we will still like them as we begin to see what is beneath their best self.

PATTERNS AND RED FLAGS

It's such a pity that hindsight is only available after the event. However, we can use it to reflect on what we missed earlier in the relationship. What red flags did your ex-partner show early on that you missed or chose to ignore? Take a moment to re-examine their personality traits, behaviours and habits. What about these irritated you? Don't worry about being judgemental—this exercise is for your self-awareness—it's not about them.

For example, did you ignore signs that they had an introverted nature which could clash with your social butterfly personality? What about tidiness—were you on the same page? Was their untidiness or being obsessively tidy a red flag? Was your need for punctuality compromised when your partner took ages to get ready to go out? What really got to you? Where did you turn a blind eye or feel rejected when hints were ignored? Would you notice this red flag and act differently in the future?

By doing this exercise, you may see similar patterns in former relationships. This may be due to feeling not good enough or being seen as the price to pay to stay in the relationship. Is this true for you? Another reason behind acceptance of poor behaviour might be dissociation learnt from earlier painful events. Dissociation may also blank out relationship lessons from painful break-ups, which can lead to repeatedly making the same mistakes. This might look like this: Susanna dates Tom, then later Dick, and afterwards Harry. These men appear different, yet underneath the surface, their similar poor behaviour keeps triggering Susanna. She recognises something isn't working, but her dissociation clouds the lessons. She misses vital clues and potentially does not change her behaviour either. And so the cycle continues.

Being conscious of significant red flags means you will spot them more easily. Everyone has some bad habits and characteristics. Which of them are not acceptable to you in a future relationship? Remember, you are good enough just as you are. Even when your less-than-best self shows up, it's not OK to be treated disrespectfully. Relationships need compromise, but it should not always be you giving in to your partner's needs.

LOOKING FOR THE REASONS

The greatest reason for being in a relationship has nothing to do with sex—as fantastic as that can be. Nor is it the thoughtful cup of tea in bed, the kisses and cuddles on the sofa, or the companionship. The primary but largely hidden reason why we enter and stay in an intimate relationship is to be fully seen and accepted—just as we are. This is the self who is kind, caring, courageous and vulnerable but also afraid and, on occasion, mean-spirited, selfish and not telling the whole truth. To be accepted for all of who we are, not just our best self. To see ourselves in the mirror our partner holds for us—this is the greatest gift of being a couple. Losing this precious space to be fully yourself hurts when your relationship ends.

When my husband and I went our separate ways, the reasons were not obvious. We rarely argued, and there wasn't anyone else involved, so when people asked me why we broke up, I said we had fallen out of love, and he didn't understand me. This last bit about not being understood, effectively laid the blame at his door. It took me a long time to see that understanding one another is a two-way street. When I finally asked myself the deeper questions about our break-up, I had to face how I blocked my husband from seeing the real me. And, because of all the other stuff going on at the end of our time together, I didn't fully understand him either. By blaming my ex-husband, I abdicated myself from my role in the breakdown of our marriage. Would knowing this at the time have changed anything? Probably not, as it wasn't that simple. However, I hope my awareness now makes me more honourable when relationships hit a rough patch.

Looking for reasons why things went pear-shaped also means looking at our role in the relationship. What baggage did we bring with us? Did we take the easy route when things were difficult? Or blame our partner when part of it lay with us?

In the chapter, *Restoring Your Boundaries*, Angie and Jack's relationship was based on their daughter Katy. They were not a good match on so many levels, and both sides had broken boundaries. Were you a good match, or did you stay together because of your children or for financial or other mutually beneficial reasons?

Poor communication and taking each other for granted are the most common reasons a relationship falls apart. Not being heard or seen is often the reason for affairs too. Some break-ups result from feeling worlds apart, having cultural differences, or wanting to follow different dreams. And there are hidden drivers that can cause a break-up—these often have ties to past trauma.

Mark, one of my past clients, easily attracted girlfriends, but his relationships were always short-lived. Discovering the real reason why this kept happening was quite a surprise.

MARK'S STORY

To the outside world, Mark's life looked great. As a professional footballer with a generous salary, he had bought a beautiful apartment overlooking Bournemouth beach. He drove a Spider sports car, and his recent goal-scoring successes had attracted the interest of several higher-league clubs. He told me he had everything he wanted, apart from the woman of his dreams.

Good-looking, fit and on the fringes of fame, Mark had no problem attracting girls—yet his longest relationship had only lasted eight months. At the club, Mark's teammates ribbed him—*a new girl every time we win!*—and Mark laughed to hide his embarrassment and frustration. He was, he told me, ready to meet 'the one', get married and raise a family. He didn't understand why things always went wrong, although he had sussed there was a pattern.

'I'm drawn to caring girls. Beautiful girls—but girls that care about the real me—not Mark, the footballer.'

Mark told me his relationships started well. Forever optimistic, he would impulsively buy her extravagant gifts.

'Perhaps I'm a bit OTT, but I like spoiling my girl.'

In the beginning, it was always the same. The new girlfriend seemed caring and made him feel special, and Mark was happy. However, after a few months, in Mark's eyes, their behaviour changed. Increasingly, his girlfriend would ask for favours—like free tickets for friends—or ask him to do things for her that he felt were unreasonable.

'I want to be the nice guy—not selfish. But the way they ask sounds demanding. It makes me want to pull away.'

Soon, one of two things would happen. Either Mark would break-up with the girl because he increasingly felt trapped, or he would become so unavailable that his girlfriend ended their relationship. No matter who broke up with whom, on the day it happened, Mark felt relieved. Yet a day or two later, he felt miserable because he felt he had once again failed.

Delving deeper into his story, Mark told me he didn't know his dad—he had left when he was two. Tracking his dad down had crossed his mind, but he knew it would upset his mum. Besides, his dad had not cared for him, so Mark had pushed his curiosity away. When he was younger, his mum had worked as a bookkeeper Monday to Friday and at the local pub on Saturday nights. Having little time for Mark, he felt unloved.

'I get it now, but her nagging when I was a teenager drove me crazy. *Do your homework. Tidy your room. Help with the washing.* Endless demands and no time for fun.' Mark sighed. 'Sometimes she'd yell and scream at me when she was drunk. I couldn't cope, so I'd just get out of the house and stay out 'til dark.'

Sensing this might be a pattern, I asked, 'Perhaps there is a connection between your reaction to your mum's demands and how you feel when your girlfriends ask favours?'

Mark shrugged, 'I don't think so. It was just a teenage thing.'

I asked him to visualise himself as a fourteen-year-old. What did he like to wear? How was his hair styled?

'Can you see your teenage self?' I asked.

Mark, with his eyes closed, nodded.

'Now, see your mum nagging you to do your homework. What do you see?'

Mark's closed eyelids fluttered.

'Mum is angry with me. I'm not good enough. She wants me to do well at school to get a well-paid job. I feel scared of Mum's anger—like I'm a little boy—but I'm taller and stronger than her.'

Opening his eyes, he was for a moment silent, and I waited while he processed these realisations. Then a wry smile crossed his face, 'When I was upset, I'd go outside to kick my football against the house. I kept kicking the ball, over and over sometimes for an hour or more. That thumping must have driven Mum crazy, but she rarely complained. I guess that's how I coped with the unspoken stuff.'

His smile softened as he added. 'I can see it was tough for us both, but Mum's sober now, and we're good.'

We went on to analyse the negative personality traits of Mark's former girlfriends—those who had lasted longer than the others. Of course, everyone has good and not-so-good characteristics, but focusing on the negative ones highlights common threads. This exercise revealed that often the girls expressed their anger by shouting at him. He also realised that many were insecure too.

Honing in on the insecurity, I asked Mark whether—in a backhanded way—the girlfriends asking a lot might be driven by their insecurities? Were they trying to feel safe by having you do things for them? Did his pulling away perhaps make them feel less secure in the relationship, leading them to become more demanding of his time?

Mark had made many assumptions about the girls' behaviour but had not considered this. Mark realised he was surprisingly shy about sharing his feelings and lacked curiosity about his girlfriend's behaviour. Slowly, Mark began to put the pieces of his jigsaw together.

The different perspectives held about Mark's love life are interesting to see. To his teammates, Mark was just one of the lads, not serious about any girl. For the girlfriends, I imagine they were perplexed why things with Mark started so well and then quickly went downhill. While for Mark, in stark contrast to his football career, he felt like a failure in the world of romance.

Sometimes, the real reason for a relationship not working out is hidden. Might there be more to your break-up too?

BE PROACTIVE ABOUT ANY LONELINESS

After a long time of togetherness, it's natural to miss your partner, even if you are angry with them. Going to bed alone after years of snuggling can be challenging. The desire to talk to them can be overwhelming. Remember, though, there was a reason for this break-up. So, resist the temptation to call, show-up unannounced on their doorstep or brush everything under the rug. If the relationship has fully broken down, trying to keep it alive simply prolongs the time it takes to heal.

When the biggest waves of pain have subsided, reconnect with friends and attend social events. This may not be the time for partying, but gently re-entering into social life as a singleton may be more fun than you supposed. Fight the urge to quickly sign up on dating apps too. Make sure your grieving is complete before beginning a relationship dance with someone new.

EXERCISES TO HEAL AND LET GO

The following questions ask you to dig deeper to see the bigger picture of your relationship and the break-up. Don't rush for instant answers—instead, allow your thoughts to percolate. Doing this will enable you to let go more easily and be open to what comes next for you. Write your answers now. Later reflect on them, and you can either add to them or revise them as feels right.

* List three irritating, infuriating behaviours or habits of your ex-partner.
* Name three areas where, recently, your ex-partner was increasingly not on the same page. For example, *We had increasingly different*

views about money. I wanted us to have savings to feel safe, but he believed that credit cards are for enjoying life today. When he booked exotic holidays that we couldn't afford, I didn't enjoy them because I was too worried about how much it all cost.

* Does your ex-partner have similar negative traits to those in earlier relationships?

* Name one red flag that you won't ignore in the future.

* Flip the coin. Write about three wonderful times you shared together.

* Which of your traits did your ex-partner moan or grumble about? Do any of these need self-improvement work?

* Write a few lines about what hurts you most about your break-up.

* In a future relationship, I will prioritise... (choose a value that is important to you).

* Write a paragraph that begins: I am grateful to [ex-partner's name] for... Make sure it includes at least five things, and expand on why you are grateful for their journey with you. This is a tough exercise because when we are hurt all we focus on is their shadow side, not their light. So, dig deep. There are many things for which you can be grateful. The more you can write, the easier it is to release your ex-partner with love and wish them well for their onward journey through life.

Well done for completing the above exercise. When you look at this again, perhaps in a few months, notice what has changed. Trust that when you are ready another man or woman will come into your life, and it may be the best dance you have ever experienced!

Mourning loss and the journey through grief

There is a sacredness in tears.
They are not the mark of weakness, but of power.
They speak more eloquently than ten thousand tongues.
They are messengers of overwhelming grief and unspeakable love.
♥ Washington Irving

We rarely speak about dying or grief. For most of us, the thought of losing a loved one is too scary to contemplate. As for our mortality—that's not something we ever want to consider. So, we push our fears of death and grieving aside and blindly hope that when the time comes, we will have the strength to deal with it then.

Despite not wanting to consider death and loss, they are part of life, and we will grieve many times. We will mourn the loss of our parents—sometimes grieving before they die as illness robs them of who they were. There may be sudden, unexpected or shocking deaths of family members or friends. And other losses like a dear friendship that is no more, the loss of a job, perhaps a divorce, or even the loss of our own health.

THE EMOTIONAL TURMOIL OF GRIEF

To fully grieve, we have to get past our intellect. We have to feel everything. It doesn't help to wallow in grief, nor is it helpful to suppress our feelings.

In virtually all cases, we can't bypass the heart-aching sadness that initially comes up with grief either. And with this sadness, there will be a potent mix of other emotions, which may include feeling angry, depressed, overwhelmed, confused, hurt, lost, regretful, guilty or numb. Offered a choice, we would give a wide berth to such feelings. And yet when grief arrives at our door, we have to allow ourselves to embark on the journey ahead. Allowing the emotions to flow will reveal their insights and messages, healing the loss and taking us through a form of rebirth.

Throughout your grieving, sometimes at inconvenient moments, tears may suddenly fill your eyes. Or tears may roll unbidden down your cheeks, or you may end up in a heap of messy sobs. You may lose your appetite or eat anything that doesn't require preparation, cooking, or attention. Sleep may be elusive, or you sleep so deeply that it takes a massive effort to get out of bed every day. Work may suddenly seem irrelevant, or you become totally engrossed in it because it blocks out the pain. Grief may make you more reflective or restless or make you want to live recklessly. Often, it's only after you have re-found some inner peace that you realise the depth and breadth of your grieving journey.

No one can determine the length of grieving—it can take weeks, months, a year or even longer. Mainly it is determined by the closeness of your relationship with the deceased. Or if the grief is not about a death, then the importance to you of what has been lost. Each period of grieving may be different from the one before. Yet, even when the emotional turmoil is difficult to process, it's never constant. There are always waves of these feelings.

Initially, after the death of someone you love, it can feel like you are at sea in a small boat whose engine isn't working properly. The sea is wild, and waves toss the boat around as if it is nothing more than a matchstick. For ages it is like being lost at sea, unable to fathom how to get back to shore. Almost at the point where it's too much to bear, the boat engine splutters back to life. Slowly you make some progress, yet still out of the blue comes another wave knocking you sideways. Eventually, the waves lessen, and finally your boat makes it safely into the harbour.

While grieving, we are sometimes unable to express the turmoil of emotions we feel inside. Grief can show up as feeling numb, and perhaps unable to shed a single tear. When this happens, the outside world may believe we are cold or unaffected. But this is rarely true. The death of a loved one can be so overwhelming that we cannot process that which is hidden deep inside. If this resonates with you, trust that you can still travel through your grief and reach the other side. It may, though, take a little longer.

MY STORY: GRIEVING THE LOSS OF MY PARENTS

Before my dad died ten years ago, I thought I understood grief. I had read articles on Google as well as a couple of books on the process of grieving. My research was mainly to help clients still struggling with their grief as part of other things going on for them. But it wasn't until Dad died, when I felt the loss, anguish and profound sadness, that I fully knew grief. Then, after Mum died, I discovered grief could be different from my earlier experience.

Deciding whether or not to share my story of grieving has been challenging. This section was like a hokey-cokey dance—I put it in, edited it out, rewrote, and then put it back in again. Eventually, I realised sharing this story was to show the depth of grief experienced before my parents' deaths as much as afterwards. People are living longer, yet the quality of their life may not be good at the end. Coping with your parents' demise is distressing and challenging for everyone in the family.

Dad was diagnosed with Parkinson's when he was seventy-three—not that old, really. He was still full of wanderlust and was planning the next off-the-beaten-track location to photograph another rare bird. Mum had long ago given up the idea of beach holidays and mostly enjoyed their shared adventures—even when it meant using primitive bathroom facilities. Dad had joked that he would reassess his travel plans when he was eighty-five, so the diagnosis was a shock. Dad hid his sadness and dismay, knowing this diagnosis would curtail future travel plans. Dad's stoicism was much the same when six weeks later he found out he had lymphoma. Towards the end of his life, his doctors told us that Dad also had the beginnings of Alzheimer's.

Even in the early days of his illness, Dad rarely spoke about losing his physical and mental capabilities. Whenever I asked him how he was doing, his response invariably was, *I'm OK. My neck hurts a bit.* He also accepted the hassle and tiring trips to the hospital without complaint. He hated it when he could no longer drive, and as his illness progressed, in unfamiliar places, Dad would quickly lose his bearings and wander off.

Mum struggled with Dad's decline. Increasingly she was his carer, and she too had health issues. It was exhausting for her when Dad could no longer be of assistance with household chores. After a great deal of persuasion from me and my sisters, Mum finally accepted a carer to help Dad with his personal care. Mum would regale the carers with stories of Dad's earlier life and his many achievements as they helped him to shower, shaved him and eased his stiff limbs into his clothes. She wanted them to know Dad for who he had been and not the shadow of the man he had become.

After four years of various cancer treatments, Dad's monthly chemotherapy began to take so much out of him that he would sleep all day long for the week afterwards. The time came when it felt wrong to keep making Dad feel worse when there was no cure. So, we asked the doctors to stop the treatments. For the next two months, Dad appeared better than he had been for a while.

As that summer faded, and knowing Dad might not have much longer, I visited my parents more often. On Dad's better days, we would walk around his magnificent garden. Dad shuffled along on the paths in his slippers—the shuffling is a symptom of Parkinson's. We went slowly and often stopped because walking took a lot out of Dad. We admired the waterfall and the stream that ran down to the huge pond that Dad had dug out with small digger. The trees he had planted were now fully matured, and his lavender hedge and the beautiful flower beds attracted bees and butterflies. Once, this land had been a farmyard. Dad's vision and hard work had transformed it into a place of beauty.

On one of our walks, I asked, 'What bit of the garden are you the proudest of, Dad?'

He pointed to the tree growing awkwardly between huge boulders that made up the waterfall. The tree's branches curved towards the water, making it look like the rocks and the water had always been there.

'It planted itself,' he said, and smiled. Perhaps he was remembering the day he hired a full-sized JCB digger to move tons of stone to form this waterfall. Or perhaps Dad's thought simply came from us standing close to the tree, and seeing it, gave him a moment of joy.

In September, I received a call from my sister saying Dad wasn't doing so well. I quickly packed a bag and jumped into my car. When I arrived at my parents' home, Dad was asleep in his recliner chair next to the large patio overlooking the garden. I gently kissed his head, not wanting to wake him, and then had a cup of tea with Mum. We talked about everything, apart from Dad not having long to live.

The next morning, Mum, Dad and I sat at the kitchen table, all of us still in pyjamas. Dad spread his toast with a thick slab of butter and lashings of marmalade and tucked in with gusto. After breakfast, as Mum and I cleared the table, Dad's carer called. She apologised profusely, saying she was unable to come that morning. I asked Dad whether it was OK for me to help him. He simply said yes. As he sat on the shower stool and I gently soaped his body, I realised the act of me caring for him in this way felt like completing the cycle of life when decades ago he had cared for me.

Two days later, Dad died peacefully in his bed. Mum, one of my sisters and me were at his side. He was seventy-eight, but he had crammed so much into his years. With Mum, they had built a business from scratch and had sixty employees. Dad was twice president of the local Rotary Club. And in following his passion for bird photography, Dad and Mum had travelled to every continent, including Antarctica, where he took amazing photos of icebergs and penguins. Dad had loved us all and moved heaven and earth for us to be happy.

Because Dad had gradually slipped away, with relatively little drama, we all had the chance to speak about everything we wanted or needed to say. People talk of having a good death. I'm not sure how to define that, but I think Dad's passing was as good as it could have been for him, and for that, I am grateful.

After the whirlwind of Dad's funeral, my sisters and I helped Mum to move into a new home in a retirement estate. I thought I would be OK. Sad, of course. Missing him, yes, but I wasn't prepared for how grief would tear my heart out. Tears behind my eyes came from nowhere, often triggered when I saw a beautiful nature scene. These places brought up memories of Dad with his camera slung around his neck as he tried to get just the right angle for his photographs. And in these moments, the ache of still wanting to share things with him left me feeling bereft and lost.

Soon after the funeral, I began working again, helping clients struggling with their difficulties. With my professional hat on, I could temporarily put my grief on hold. But the distance-learning course on Naturopathic Nutrition, which I was midway through, suffered. Initially sympathetic, my tutors soon became frustrated with the tardiness of my coursework assignments. I knew my excuses were lame, but I still felt overwhelmed. It felt like my brain was too foggy to absorb and process new information.

Struggling to deal with my grief for Dad, I looked for answers in my books and on Google. I kept bumping into the *Five Stages of Grief* described by Swiss psychiatrist Elisabeth Kübler-Ross in her 1969 book, *On Death and Dying*. I wondered whether I was stuck in one of these stages. The stages were listed as denial, anger, bargaining, grief and acceptance. I checked in with myself. Did I feel any sense of denial? Dad's death had hovered on the horizon for a long time as his health deteriorated. No, denial didn't resonate. Was I angry with Dad, myself or anyone else? No, that too didn't tally with my feelings. By the time I considered bargaining, I had mentally given up trying to find more answers.

There wasn't an exact date when I found peace with Dad's passing—my guess it was probably around a year after his death. I still miss him, but now my memories are from before he was ill. He was my rock, and I remember his passion for nature, photography and travel and his playful sense of fun. Most of all, I'm grateful that he was my dad.

Having made this journey through grief, I thought I knew what to expect with Mum's decline in health and later her death—but it was very different.

Since her mid-fifties, Mum had struggled with her health after being diagnosed with Myasthenia gravis (Myasthenia) and Neuromyotonia. These rare auto-immune diseases affect the muscles, and Myasthenia, in particular, affects the eyes and throat. In the beginning, the most noticeable impact was tiredness and double vision. There wasn't—isn't—a cure for either condition, but medication helps. Mum's doctors told her she would probably die with these illnesses rather than of them, which was sort-of correct.

Not long after Dad's death, Mum became less steady on her feet. Initially, she didn't want to use a walking stick or a walker until the number of falls became scary for her and for my sisters and me. Nor did Mum wish to give up driving until she had a crash, which quickly led to the sale of her car and the purchase of a mobility scooter. After a particularly nasty fall resulting in a broken pelvis, Mum begrudgingly accepted the help of a carer. However, once she could use her walker again, she cancelled the contract my sisters had set up for her.

Over the next few years, Mum's feisty need for independence made her want to do everything herself. My sisters, who lived nearby, increasingly needed to step in more often. They ferried her to doctors and hospital appointments, took her on clothes shopping trips, and regularly cooked meals for her. I called Mum most days, often feeling guilty that my sisters were doing the hard work. I lived too far away to offer much practical help or lighten my sisters' load.

In 2020, Mum was eighty-two. That year, Mothering Sunday was March 22nd, the day before Boris Johnson delivered his message, *You must stay at home*. Rumours of a lockdown were rife, and I decided to visit Mum. Mostly, I wanted to be with her on Mothering Sunday, but I also needed to talk with my sisters. *What would we do if the lockdown happened?* We decided that no matter what Boris would say on Monday, Mum couldn't manage without some outside help, and we would provide that, even if it meant breaking the law.

On that Sunday afternoon, with my car packed, Mum and I were sitting in the lounge having a final cup of tea. It was time to go. I got up, leaned down to Mum, who was sitting in her armchair, and I hugged her.

'I don't want to leave, but if there's going to be a lockdown, I can't stay here. I'll let you know when I get home.'

She hugged me back and then surprised me with, 'Are you scared we might not see one another again?'

I stood up, looked at her and nodded, unable to reply as tears filled my eyes.

Then with unusual clarity, she added, 'I'm scared too. But if this is the last time we see one another, remember I'm proud of you, and I love you. Drive safely.'

When Dad was alive, when it was time for me to leave, Mum always came to the front door to wave me off. Getting up from her chair now took considerable effort, so we said our goodbyes in the lounge. But on this day, as I got into my car, I saw she had come to the door. We waved to one another as I drove away. Tears now rolled down my cheeks unchecked. I felt a huge lump in my throat as I wondered what would happen to Mum.

In May 2020, despite my sisters and Mum's carers being gowned, gloved and masked, Mum caught Covid. An ambulance arrived to take her to hospital. No visitors were allowed, so my sisters and I took turns calling her on her mobile. Listening to Mum's long bouts of coughing and gasping breaths on a mobile phone was a harrowing experience. Sometimes after a coughing fit, there was silence. Had Mum put her mobile phone down? Was she OK? I'd ask, *Mum, are you still there?* praying that I hadn't just heard her last breath. Eventually, I'd hear her gently moan or begin coughing again. I ended our calls with *I love you—I'll call you tomorrow.* My sisters and I never knew whether our calls were the last time we would speak to her. We all felt utterly helpless. Phoning her was the only thing we could do to let her know she wasn't alone.

Due to Mum's age and her auto-immune diseases, we knew her chances of survival were slim. But, against the odds, Mum began to improve. Her doctors removed the oxygen tubes from her nose, and two weeks later, an ambulance took Mum to a smaller hospital for recovery. One month later, Mum came back home. No longer able to walk, my sisters were shocked to see how frail she had become.

In readiness for Mum's return, we arranged for live-in carers to stay with her. Each carer would stay for three to four weeks, after which a new carer would take over. When a new carer arrived, Mum instantly disliked them until the next changeover, when often Mum would want the carer who had just left!

The carers worked hard to help Mum strengthen her muscles, and after a few weeks she could walk to a neighbour's wall, where the residents of the retirement estate met, carefully distanced, to gossip and drink coffee from flasks.

To help her move around her home, on the tray of her inhouse walker, I had written,

Breathe

Bum in

Chest out

You CAN walk!

The effort it took Mum to get out of her armchair to use her walker was enormous. Her arms would shake, and her face grimaced as she pulled herself up to standing. Yet, in the middle of the night, Mum often managed to get out of bed alone and sometimes even made it to the bathroom. Post-it notes festooned every surface around her bed with the message *Ring The Bell*. Perhaps Mum didn't want to disturb her carer's sleep; more likely it was her desire for independence. Once out of bed, Mum's legs would buckle. Her falls bruised or grazed her legs, back and arms.

Mum began to get confused about the days and often forgot the name of her latest carer. At this point, she was aware that her memory was not so good, so she scribbled reminders into her diary, but these entries later made little sense to her or to us. Mum was becoming wobblier, even with her walker. On several occasions, her carer orchestrated a controlled fall. This action stopped Mum from injuring herself, but she was almost a dead weight to lift back up from sitting on the floor. The carer would then call one of my sisters to come over to help her back on to her feet. Sadly, we realised that Mum required more help than we could provide and decided she needed to go into a care home.

My sisters drove Mum to the place we had chosen. Getting the car as close to the front door as possible, they helped Mum steady herself with the walker. Then Mum slowly walked to and through the door held open by one of the Care Home staff. Due to Covid restrictions, my sisters weren't allowed into the building. The carers took Mum to a room none of us had seen to begin her two weeks of quarantine. Not able to leave her room during this time, Mum's ability to walk once more declined.

Many thousands of families with relatives in care homes during the pandemic struggled with restricted visiting. More than the official lockdowns, care homes would shut their doors when a resident or staff member tested positive and stay closed until everyone tested negative. On one occasion, we were unable to see Mum for six weeks. Not being able to see her, not even to visit her behind a plastic screen, was beyond awful.

To stay in touch with Mum, we used FaceTime. She loved it when she could see her grandchildren and great-grandchildren. Then she began to struggle with how to use her iPad. Later still, she could no longer fathom how to use her mobile phone. Feeling cut off from Mum in every possible way, my sisters and I would call the care home for updates. Often their response was, *Your mum is fine.* Fine?! Mum was not fine in any sense of the word. Slowly we realised they meant, *Your mum is much the same as before. She hates being shut in her room—we hate it too—but we must follow Government guidelines to keep your mum and everyone safe.*

In October 2021, the care home called. *Your mum is not very well. Perhaps you can come?* My sisters were, on that day, flying home from a golfing holiday, and I set off from Portland. *Please, God, let one of us be with her before she dies.* I tried not to drive recklessly in my haste to get to Leicestershire.

I felt shaky as I was buzzed in via the glass sliding doors of the care home. I showed them my lateral flow test results, and they waved me through the security doors. Opening the door to Mum's room, I could see she was in bed, her eyes closed. The head of her hospital-type bed was titled up to ease her breathing.

'Hey Mum, how are you feeling? We have been worried about you.'

I silently chastised myself for asking such a dumb question as I said hello to my aunt who sat beside her. There is a 17-year age gap between my mum and her sister, and just 5 years between us. Growing up, my aunt was like an older sister to me. She had been sitting with Mum since early morning. She looked exhausted and I sensed she was relieved that I had arrived.

During my long drive, I had imagined Mum looking poorly, perhaps coughing incessantly as she did with Covid. I was ready to face the worse. Instead, Mum looked much like she did on my last visit two weeks before.

My sisters arrived, looking flushed from their rush from the airport. In the corridor outside Mum's room, we found another couple of chairs and squeezed around her bed. Drained from her vigil, my aunt said goodbye to her sister, unsure if this was for the last time.

Mum slipped in and out of sleep. By mid-afternoon, she had become more aware and seemed surprised to see us all in her room. As the hours passed, we caught up on our collective news, wondering if this was Mum's time. But by late evening, Mum was sleeping more peacefully, so we left, asking the care home to call if there was any change.

I stayed that night with my middle sister. In the morning, the care home called to say Mum had had a restful night. I drove over to see her and found her propped up in her bed, looking brighter and not coughing as much. I stayed with her for an hour, then drove back to Portland, wondering how to process such uncertainty about Mum's health.

The care home now classed Mum as being at the end of life, and they thankfully lifted our visiting restrictions. For some of these later visits, Mum was reasonably lucid, and we laughed at our shared memories. Occasionally, Mum would complain about this and that—usually about one of the carers—but then would smile beatifically when one of them popped in to see her. Then there were times when Mum slept for the full forty-five minutes of the allotted visiting time. By now, even on the good days, my sisters and I knew she would probably soon forget that we had visited.

By mid-January 2022, Mum could no longer eat or drink unaided. Her doctor said that the Myasthenia now made swallowing difficult, and there was a possibility of choking. He decided Mum should no longer receive food, water, or medication, but the carers would administer hourly mouth care, a procedure that involves moistening the mouth with a tiny damp cloth. The doctor's decision was shocking and heart-breaking, but Mum was living a ghastly form of existence. My sisters and I considered other equally awful options, and, with deep sadness, we agreed to follow the doctor's advice.

Mum's doctor had said she might live for three or four more days but then added that you can never tell for sure. After the third day, Mum was no longer conscious. My sisters and I took turns holding her hand, talking to her, and we chatted to one another as the hours slowly ticked by. We tuned her radio to Classic FM, which she used to love, and we waited.

Day six came and went, and now my sister and I were practically living in the care home. We took turns sleeping on the floor or in Dad's old reclining chair next to Mum's bed. When the waiting became unbearable, one of us would go for a walk in the nearby park and buy snacks to keep us going. Were those days of waiting with Mum to help us all? To help Mum's soul accept that her death was close and to help my sisters and me with our grieving process? Perhaps—but the waiting was agony.

After ten days of no sustenance, Mum suddenly stopped breathing. I have to admire how her spirit battled on to the end. After Mum's final breath my sister and I hugged one another. We were exhausted and also relieved. Admitting to the relief feels horrible, but the rollercoaster of the last two years had taken a massive toll on all of the family.

I miss my mum. Not as she was at the end, but Mum as she was before her health deteriorated. I still want to call her to share my news. And although it's illogical, I can't yet bring myself to delete her mobile number or our WhatsApp messages from my phone.

Unlike after Dad's death, there have only been a few tears. I have felt more numb than anything else. I also feel restless and want to do something new, yet I don't know what that is. I continue to sit with my grief, knowing more emotions may come up or that maybe this time it was internally processed long before her death.

I recently caught myself singing along to a song on the radio while driving and realised that I hadn't done that for ages. Like the snowdrops in my garden announcing spring, life goes on, and it feels like joy is once more in the air for me.

THE REAL MEANING OF THE FIVE STAGES OF GRIEF

To write this chapter, I returned to the idea of the five stages of grief, identified by Elisabeth Kübler-Ross's work on different websites. I re-read some of the stages, and they still didn't make much sense. So, I finally bought her book. I was surprised to discover that the website articles had somewhat missed the point. Kübler-Ross had written her book to help doctors, nurses and families understand the grief people felt at the end of their life—not the grief felt by a bereavement.

Kübler-Ross and her team had interviewed over two hundred patients at the University of Chicago Hospital. These interviews highlighted a pattern of grieving phases that almost all patients experienced as they faced their mortality. Kübler-Ross classified these as stages and shared her findings in her book. She emphasised that not everyone experienced all of these stages, which could happen out of sequence or overlap.

I read that denial and isolation—the first stage—is nearly always accompanied by hope. This stage often shows up when a patient does not want to accept the prognosis. Or they are adamant that their results are for another Mr J Smith—not for them. Or they hope for a miracle cure because they do not wish to accept how little time they have left.

Understanding this, I can now see how Mum battled against her diagnosis and, later, her physical decline. Until almost the end, Mum hoped her doctors would prescribe new medication that would make her better.

Kübler-Ross witnessed anger in many of the patients she interviewed. Most felt it was too soon for them to die, that it wasn't fair that this was happening. They often felt frustrated that their body wasn't functioning as it once did. Nearly always, their anger was tinged with regret. They didn't want to miss life's milestones, like walking a daughter down the aisle or being there for the arrival of a grandchild. They still wanted to complete their dreams, and it was hard for them to accept this was now impossible.

Mum always told my sisters and me she didn't want a prolonged death. For decades she supported Dignity in Dying and Dignitas. Yet, simultaneously, she was frustrated that her body and mind didn't work the way she wanted. I think it was her eternal hope that kept her alive much longer than she or we expected.

During the bargaining stage, those facing death often plead with doctors, family or God for more months or to do something they love just one more time.

The fourth stage identified by Kübler-Ross is grief, which shows up similarly to feelings felt after the death of someone close. With Mum, this stage was never constant. There were days, especially towards the end, when yes, she was despondent, yet mostly Mum kept her sadness under wraps. That, in part, was down to her personality and perhaps part of her generation's attitude of keeping calm and carrying on.

Dad didn't speak about dying, yet at the very end, I sensed that he had come to terms with it and accepted this was his time. By contrast, Mum did not accept what was happening to her. During our last real conversation, on New Year's Day, I said, 'It will be your birthday soon, Mum. You'll be eighty-four, and I'll soon be sixty-four. How old we have become,' I teased her.

I rattled on because Mum was half asleep. 'Do you remember The Beatles song, Mum—*When I'm sixty-four*?' and I softly sang the first verse.

I paused. 'Mum, is there anything that you would like for your birthday?'

'I don't think I'll bother with my birthday,' she muttered with her eyes still closed.

I didn't know how to respond. Mum was existing—not living. More than anything, I knew she would have loved for her family—all of us—to be with her one last time, but due to Covid, that was impossible to arrange. She hadn't met her three latest great-grandchildren. I was suddenly filled with sorrow that her amazing life was ending in such an abysmal way.

Perhaps deep down Mum already knew her end was close because she died three days before her birthday.

Does grief after a death go through these five stages too? Perhaps for some people it does. If it helps you see the phases you are passing through, that's good. But don't worry if they don't resonate. Handling your grief doesn't need labels—it's more important that you find a way that helps you through your journey of grief.

HOW OUR APPROACH TO DEATH HAS EVOLVED

The Victorians talked openly and frequently about death because early deaths were not uncommon. From a young age, people would plan and inform their families about their wishes for their passing. They also began saving money early on to cover the high funeral expenses of the time.

Greatly influenced by Queen Victoria's mourning for Albert, a complex set of rules emerged. Manuals instructed people on funeral etiquette, including set times for grieving, and dictated what should be worn. Widows, during the first year, were to wear a plain black dress without any jewellery. They could not socialise with others apart from on Sundays, when they were allowed to attend church. During the second year, a widow could wear dresses in shades of grey or lavender. Widowers had an easier time. They simply had to wear black gloves and a black band around their hat for six months. Victorians feared upsetting society, and so they avidly followed the prescribed rules.

In my grandma's time, women still used to wear black for one year and a day to mark the passing of their husbands. Now even wearing black for funerals is less common as people choose to celebrate the life of the one who has died as opposed to mourning their death. A day or two after a funeral, most people have to return to work. It can be challenging to express our feelings to others without any visible indication that we are still grieving. It's also difficult for others to remember that we may not be our usual selves.

WHEN WE GET STUCK IN GRIEF

There are situations when grieving stalls or may not even begin. The shock from a sudden or unexpected death can shut us down. Traumatic deaths where others died but you survived may also trigger survivor's guilt. In cases like this, or when grief remains incomplete or trapped, it can feel impossible to move on. Symptoms of unprocessed, lingering grief can manifest as lethargy, depression and anxiety. These were symptoms that occurred for another client—Lily.

LILY'S STORY

Many years ago, as a newbie Life Coach, I was asked to help a friend of a friend, an elderly lady called Lily. We worked on the phone and never met in person. Despite living in Dorset for over forty years, Lily still had a broad

Yorkshire accent. She also had that rare ability to poke fun at herself and make others laugh with her.

During our first call, Lily told me about her husband Charlie's death. I heard how one morning, three years ago, Charlie kissed her goodbye, winked and teasingly said, *See ya later, alligator*. He had picked up his car keys and left for the short drive to his office. Less than an hour later, Lily made the same journey. There she found him on the floor, beside his desk, looking for all the world like he had just fallen asleep. A doctor later told Lily that Charlie had had a massive heart attack and died instantly.

'He was my friend and dancing partner. I miss 'im. 'Ow do you get over it?'

There was a short silence as she regained her composure, and I expressed my condolences for her loss. Then I asked Lily why our mutual friend was concerned for her well-being.

'Well, my house is a bloody mess,' she said and burst into laughter.

She sighed, and her joy vanished into thin air.

'Charlie would wonder what the 'ell was the matter with me,' she said. 'I know I should do somethin' about it, but I can't.'

I gentled probed and discovered Lily's home had stuff everywhere. Sitting on her piano was a stack of unopened envelopes—mostly brown ones that looked like bills—and piles of books. On the kitchen table were plates, pots and pans. She told me after washing up that she couldn't be bothered to put them away. It had become a habit to leave them there. In her bedroom, an armchair was draped with most of her dresses because she couldn't face getting rid of Charlie's clothes, which filled over half of her wardrobe. From this, I sensed Lily might benefit from being set a specific task, so I asked; 'Would you like to play your piano again?'

'That'd be grand.'

So, I set her a challenge to move everything off the piano—and not just dump it elsewhere but find a proper place for everything. And then to play something—anything—on her piano. With a sigh, Lily accepted my suggestion.

The following week, when I called Lily, she told me she had roped in her neighbour Betty to help with the tidying project. After they had cleared everything away—admitting she had not sorted all of the envelopes—she had played a few tunes. She enjoyed it—especially playing one of Charlie's favourite songs. She added that her piano needed tuning. Before I could suggest a piano tuner, Lily said it was already sorted.

The next challenge for Lily was to tackle her bedroom, mainly to let go of Charlie's old clothes. I asked Lily to choose three of Charlie's bow ties as a reminder of their dancing days. Then, everything else could be given to family, friends or a charity shop. Lily baulked. *I can't do that!* After considering several different approaches, we found a compromise. Lily would ask her daughter to come around one evening to bag the clothes and take them away while she stayed at Betty's. The following week, Lily laughed when I asked for a progress report. She told me she had been a fool for not clearing away Charlie's clothes before now. It felt good to hang up her clothes properly once more.

Finding out more about Lily, I heard Betty would pop round most evenings. She would bring a bag of sweeties, which they munched through as they watched their favourite soaps and dramas until late. I knew Lily also watched some daytime TV and I was curious about how much time she actually spent glued to the television. So, I asked her to keep a record.

At the beginning of our next call, Lily was her usual forthright self.

'It were thirty 'ours. Thirty hours just sittin' on my bum—that's more than I worked for Charlie! Can't believe it were that much.'

I tried to fathom what watching so much TV would feel like, but before I could offer any thoughts, without pausing for a breath, Lily continued.

'Need t' stop this nonsense!'

It was one of the joys of coaching Lily. She was nearly always two steps ahead of me.

Next, I asked Lily what she used to like doing or what she might like to do. She told me that as a teenager she loved painting, but when the children came along, and later when she had worked for Charlie, there had not been time for this hobby.

Would she like to paint again? I asked.

By the following week, Lily had discovered an art class at U3A and had also persuaded Betty to join her for a line dancing class.

After months of sorting, clearing and moving, Lily began one of our calls uncharacteristically sad, 'I don't think of Charlie s'much. I feel guilty I don't.'

'That's natural,' I reassured her. 'It doesn't mean you have forgotten him. He is still in your heart.' Then I asked, 'What do you think Charlie would say about how much you've done recently?'

'About time, woman!' and Lily laughed raucously.

It would be easy to think that this approach might always work on grief that has become stuck—but that's not always true. Often when grief hasn't moved on, it needs more than just practical suggestions. Helping stuck grief to flow typically involves more talking therapy and healing. Lily, though, was ready to move forward—she just needed a nudge.

FINAL THOUGHTS ON BEREAVEMENT

Ultimately, the journey of grief after losing a loved one is both healing and challenging. It is also uniquely personal. Grief's tangled web of emotions can take us to places we didn't know before. Yet the feelings that surface provide significant insights into the nature of life, adding to our wisdom and compassion. When grieving, the following tips may help you.

* Be gentle with your soul while you grieve.

* Grieving takes time—it can't be rushed.

* It's OK to cry—let your tears flow when they come up. It's also OK if there are no tears to shed.

* Talk to friends and family about your loss and how you feel—it helps.

* It's OK if you don't experience grief as others do—trust your intuition about what is suitable for you.

* Although the person who died is no longer physically with you, they always remain in your heart, so you can still talk to them.

* For shocking, traumatic, sudden deaths, professional guidance is invaluable—there is no shame in asking for help.

* Always remember that your loved one would not wish for you to prolong your sadness and pain at their passing. As you begin to feel better, please don't fight it. It is OK for you to be happy again.

How to continue your happiness journey

You can't go back and make a new start,
but you can start right now and
make a brand new ending.
♥ James R. Sherman

Over the last few decades, I've read a huge pile of self-help books. Some, I now only vaguely remember. Others transformed my life and have become well-thumbed favourites. Those with the biggest impact on me were the ones I re-read, made notes, completed their exercises, scribbled in the margins and highlighted specific sentences. If this book has helped you—YAY!—please re-read the chapters that resonated to further enhance your understanding. Then keep this book for future reference, or pass it on to someone who may benefit from a deeper understanding of healing.

We want to believe that making changes—like being happier—can happen overnight, but such rapid changes are rare. Daily we change our beliefs, values and habits, but the shifts are typically so small as to be almost imperceptible. However, if you compare how you are today, with who you were five or ten years ago, it is easy to see how much you have changed.

Casting off yesterday's traumas takes courage, but it is a necessary part to becoming happier in life. Your journey is unique, but I encourage you to love and forgive yourself, and to keep working on the areas of your life that need attention. Remember even baby steps of doing things differently, ultimately lead to big changes to your life. You can do this!

Two more books in the *Find Your Inner Happiness* series are on their way. The second book, *Make Tomorrow Amazing,* takes a life coaching approach to happiness showing you how to create a Life Plan. While the third, *Walk Today In Peace,* provides spiritual guidance for peace and harmony in life. Please email me to hear when these are available; jennie@jenniebayliss. com. Also find more articles on my website www.jenniebayliss.com.

FIND INSPIRATIONAL WORDS

Choose words to live by—poems, quotations or specific passages—to inspire, motivate and act as your guide on your journey through life. Mine are from a short quotation by Aesop; *No act of kindness, no matter how small, is ever wasted.* I also love many of the poems and quotations by Rumi, particularly this one;

> *Try not to resist the changes that come your way. Instead let life live through you. And do not worry that your life is turning upside down. How do you know that the side you are used to is better than the one to come?*

Good places to search for such words are; www.goodreads.com and www.brainyquote.com You can also find more of my favourites at www. jenniebayliss.com/inspiring-quotations/

FIND YOUR HEROES

I believe everyone needs heroes. At the top of my list are many people who are unknown to the wider world, including my daughters. However, the following wonderfully diverse people, are also my heroes. Google can help you find their websites and books. By the way, it was impossible to rank these people, so this list is in no particular order.

- ❖ **The Dalai Lama** is the spiritual leader of the Tibetan People. Exiled from Tibet after the Chinese invasion in 1959, the Dalai Lama travels the world with messages of peace, hope and compassion—for people of all faiths. I admire his grace, wisdom, big smiles and wonderful humour.

- ❖ **Karla McLaren** is an emotional empath and author. Her understanding of the emotional realm is greater than anyone else I have come across. Karla demonstrates how our emotions dance together, to help us survive and thrive. She believes working with our feelings will restore harmony to the psyche. Her book, *The Language of Emotions—What Your Feelings are Trying to Tell You*, is still my go-to book for appreciating the nuances of our emotional world.

- ❖ **Frank Lipman** is a doctor who also trained in alternative healing, including nutrition, functional medicine, acupuncture and yoga. He runs a clinic in New York and promotes well-being through his books and videos. His book, *Spent—End Exhaustion and Feel Great Again*, radically changed my relationship with food and sleep.

- ❖ **Pema Chödrön** is a Buddhist nun trained by Tibetan monks. She teaches compassion, open-heartedness and being kind to everyone—including ourselves. Her style is humble yet playful. I love listening to her talks, particularly *Walking the Walk*, which is both profound and light-hearted.

- ❖ **Kris Carr** is an author and wellness warrior. Kris was diagnosed with a rare, incurable liver cancer in her early thirties. As part of her healing, she studied nutrition and wellness. Today she inspires others to look after their body, mind and soul. Her book, *Crazy Sexy Diet*, looks at all aspects of eating healthily. Kris's fun, kooky writing style makes you feel like she's your best friend.

- ❖ **Brené Brown** is a research professor, storyteller and author.

I watched her first TED talk and was inspired. Brené studies and teaches courage, vulnerability, shame and empathy. Her book, *The Gifts of Imperfection—Let Go of Who You Think You're Supposed to Be and Embrace Who You Are*, digs deep into the shadows of vulnerability and encourages us to live authentically.

❁ **Sadhguru** is a yogi and mystic. His passion is for teaching self-transformation without being attached to one belief system. He is pragmatic and known for answering difficult questions about how to live life in harmony with ourselves and the world.

❁ **Mike George** is an author, spiritual coach and speaker. He specialises in showing us the incongruity of our belief systems. One of his early books, *The 7 Aha!s of Highly Enlightened Souls*, and a talk in Oxfordshire made me question my beliefs and helped me to lead a more spiritual life.

❁ **Nick Ortner** is the founder of the Tapping Solution, which promotes EFT. In 2007, with the help of his sister Jessica and brother Alex, he made a documentary film called *The Tapping Solution*. This film is now available on YouTube. Nick and his family yearly host a ten-day online *Tapping World Summit*. To date, there have been more than two million attendees.

❁ **Caroline Myss** is an author, speaker and medical intuitive who speaks on human consciousness, spirituality and mysticism. Her teaching style sometimes contains home truths that are not always easy to hear, yet her work is deeply thought-provoking.

❁ **David Attenborough** is a naturalist and TV broadcaster known for his involvement in the BBC's natural world documentaries. His friendly and down-to-earth manner inspires my passion for protecting animals, plants and habitats. His recent campaign to save the fragility of the ecosystems from plastic pollution deeply touched my heart.

✤ **Brendon Burchard** is a business coach and personal development trainer. He is a force of positive energy, inspiring millions of people to succeed holistically. He has written many books, and produces videos and podcasts on personal and business development.

✤ **Patrick Holford** is a nutritionist and good health advocate. He founded the Institute of Optimum Nutrition, which teaches naturopathic nutrition. His book, *The Optimum Nutrition Bible*, was one of my course study books, which I still regularly thumb through.

✤ **Wim Hof**, known as the Ice-Man, has brought the healing power of breathing and cold therapy to the world. Wim has achieved many remarkable feats of cold endurance, including climbing Mount Kilimanjaro in shorts and sitting in an ice-cube bath for an hour. As a year-round sea swimmer, I too believe in the healing power of the cold.

✤ **Bruce Lipton** is an author and speaker. Before his spiritual awakening, he was a highly regarded Cell Biologist at Stamford University School of Medicine. His book, *The Biology of Belief*, helped me understand the science of what happens in our cells and the interaction between the subconscious and conscious mind.

✤ **Ron Siegel** is a professor of psychology at Harvard Medical School. He has a wonderfully light touch, sharing his knowledge in an easy-to-understand manner. In his clinical work, he often uses symbolism and the language of metaphor to help his clients see a broader picture. I share his beliefs in the power of this methodology.

✤ **Nick Vujicic** is an inspirational speaker. Born without limbs, he had to overcome difficulties we can't begin to imagine. His journey now inspires others to reframe obstacles as hidden opportunities.

* **Ken Wilber** is a philosopher working in the arena of transpersonal psychology. He created the concept of Integral Psychology, which weaves consciousness, spirituality, psychology and therapy together. Bringing these different ways and wisdom together makes so much sense to me.

* **Esther Perel** is a psychotherapist. I discovered her work via a TED talk. Her humour and honesty about affairs and couples therapy was like a breath of fresh air. Her work continues to inspire me to help couples who are struggling in their relationships.

* **Peter Levine** is a psychologist specialising in trauma and stress. His early work, particularly his book, *Waking the Tiger—Healing Trauma*, helped me understand how trauma resides in the body long after the event. Today, I use elements of his work to help my clients release trauma and fear energy trapped in their bodies.

* **Boyan Slat** is an inventor, entrepreneur and environmentalist. When he was eighteen, he founded *The Ocean Cleanup*—a non-profit organisation. Their specialist boats and ships are working worldwide to stop plastic from flowing from the rivers into the oceans. In 2021, they successfully began removing plastic and debris from the gigantic Garbage Patch in the Pacific Ocean.

* **Ron Finley** is an American gardening activist. In 2010, Ron decided he wanted to transform the unloved, abandoned patches of land in the poorer parts of Los Angeles into gardens. His dream was to provide vegetables and fruit to communities in food deserts— areas where supermarkets are non-existent because they have moved out of poorer areas. Ron Finley's idea has taken off in the USA. It could be a great model for the UK too.

* **Anna Jones** is a vegetarian cook and writer. She passionately promotes eating more vegetables. Her first recipe book, *A Modern Way to Eat*, is one of my favourites. I love her wonderfully honest

approach to enjoying food. Her dishes don't try to emulate meat dishes—instead, she creates fabulous plant food dishes that are exciting and delicious.

Resources

Never feel ashamed to seek help. We are living though a time of social, political and environment upheaval. These times are unsettling because mostly we don't like change. If, added into the mix, there are past traumas, it can feel like you are at the foot of a mountain with no idea how to reach the summit.

In the UK, there are thousands of counsellors, psychotherapists and alternative therapists. Recommendation from family and friends is often the best way to find someone to help you, but I wanted to provide you with a list of people and resources that I trust.

CONTACT ME - FIND OUT MORE

To contact me, please email jennie@jenniebayliss.com.

Discover more articles and advice on my website: www.jenniebayliss.com. To find out more about my retreats, please see www.thejasminehouse.com. And you can follow me on Instagram via www.instagram.com/jennie.bayliss/

To download a pdf including key exercises from this book, please go www.healyesterdaystrauma.com/free-toolkit/

MY COACHES AND HEALERS

Joel Young. Superb Emotional Healer who helped me on the early part of my journey. Founder of NPA (Non-Personal Awareness) which beautifully and simply helps you to stop taking things personally. http://www. joelyoungnpa.com

Carole Ann Rice. My brilliant Life Coach who I have worked with for 18 years. Carole Ann also runs the Pure Coaching Academy offering highly effective training for people wishing to become a Life Coach. https://www. realcoachingco.com and https://purecoachingacademy.com

Penny Waite. EFT Master and Life Coach. Penny is my go-to person when I can't see the wood for the trees. Penny's EFT mastery is second to none. https://pennywaite.co.uk

FIND SUPPORT

https://www.lifecoach-directory.org.uk
https://www.bacp.co.uk (to find Counsellors and Psychotherapists)
https://sexualabusesupport.campaign.gov.uk
https://www.nspcc.org.uk (protecting children from abuse and harm)
https://www.thetappingsolution.com (for more on EFT including tapping videos)